GREAT WAR

DERby
Remembering 1914–18

DR MIKE GALER

IN ASSOCIATION WITH DERBY MUSEUMS

The
History
Press

The author would like to thank the staff at the
Derby Local Studies Library for their help, support and patience.

First published 2014

The History Press
The Mill, Brimscombe Port
Stroud, Gloucestershire, GL5 2QG
www.thehistorypress.co.uk

© Dr Mike Galer, 2014

The right of Dr Mike Galer to be identified as the Author
of this work has been asserted in accordance with the
Copyright, Designs and Patents Act 1988.

British Library Cataloguing in Publication Data.
A catalogue record for this book is available from the British Library.

ISBN 978 0 7509 6009 0

Typesetting and origination by The History Press
Printed in Great Britain

CONTENTS

	Timeline	4
	Introduction	7
1	Outbreak of War	10
2	Preparations at Home	28
3	Work of War	49
4	News from the Front Line	72
5	Home Fires Burning	94
6	Coming Home	114
	Postscript: Legacy	130
	Sources	141
	About the Author	143

TIMELINE

1914

25 April 1914

*the last match of the 1913/1914 football season.
Derby FC draw 1–1 away at Newcastle United*

5 June 1914

*Breadsall church burns down,
allegedly due to a suffragette attack*

28 June 1914

*Assassination of Archduke
Franz Ferdinand in Sarajevo*

2 July 1914

*King George V and Queen Mary
visit Ilkeston and Heanor*

4 August 1914

Great Britain declares war on Germany

23 August 1914

Battle of Tannenberg commences

6 September 1914

First Battle of the Marne

16 October 1914

*'Call to Arms', a mass meeting in
the Royal Drill Hall, Derby, to
recruit volunteers for the war*

19 October 1914

First Battle of Ypres

1915

25 January 1915

*Inauguration of the Derbyshire
Regiment of Home Guard*

12 March 1915

*Private Jacob Rivers of Derby is killed
in action during events that led him
to be awarded the Victoria Cross*

25 April 1915

Allied landing at Gallipoli

7 May 1915

Germans torpedo and sink the Lusitania

31 May 1915

First German Zeppelin raid on London

8 August 1915

*The Derbyshire Yeomanry land
at Sulva Bay, Gallipoli*

30 October 1915

*Postwomen commence duties at Derby
as letter carriers during the war*

8 December 1915

Derby Corporation decides to employ women tram conductors for the period of the war

20 December 1915

Allies finish their evacuation of and withdrawal from Gallipoli

1916

24 January 1916

The British government introduces conscription

31 January 1916

Overnight Zeppelin raid on Derby kills four; damage to the Midland Railway Carriage and Wagon Works

21 February 1916

Battle of Verdun commences

31 May 1916

Battle of Jutland

4 June 1916

Brusilov Offensive commences

1 July 1916

First day of the Battle of the Somme, with 57,000 British casualties

27 August 1916

Italy declares war on Germany

18 December 1916

Battle of Verdun ends

1917

6 March 1917

The trial of Alice Wheeldon, pacifist and anti-war campaigner of Pear Tree Road, Derby, begins

6 April 1917

The United States declares war on Germany

9 April 1917

Battle of Arras

31 July 1917

Third Battle of Ypres (Passchendaele)

20 August 1917

Third Battle of Verdun

26 October 1917

Second Battle of Passchendaele

20 November 1917

Battle of Cambrai

7 December 1917

The United States declares war on Austria-Hungary

1918

3 March 1918

Russia and the Central Powers sign the Treaty of Brest-Litovsk

21 March 1918

Second Battle of the Somme

15 July 1918

Second Battle of the Marne

8 August 1918

Battle of Amiens, first stage of the Hundred Days Offensive

22 September 1918

The Great Allied Balkan victory

27 September 1918

Storming of the Hindenburg Line

8 November 1918

Armistice negotiations commence

9 November 1918

Kaiser Wilhelm II abdicates, Germany is declared a republic

11 November 1918

Armistice Day, cessation of hostilities on the Western Front

18 November 1918

Derby Gun Week sees displays in the Market Square

1919

30 August 1919

Football begins again with Derby FC playing at home against Manchester United, drawing 1–1

INTRODUCTION

This book is dedicated to the men and women from Derby and Derbyshire who fought, served, died and sacrificed so much in the First World War. This horrific conflict ripped the world apart and ended the hopes and dreams of a whole generation of young men and women. We, along with many other towns and cities, have the opportunity to tell the story of Derby and its people, while honouring the dead and those who survived with respect.

The war in Europe (known at the time as the Great War, or sometimes the War to End All Wars) began on 28 July 1914. Shortly after, Britain declared war on Germany, on 4 August 1914. The war officially ended in 1919 with the signing of the Treaty of Versailles on 28 June 1919, but a ceasefire was in effect from 11 November 1918.

There were many causes of the conflict which smouldered in the background for many years: naval and military expansion, especially by a belligerent Germany, challenging British superiority; the failure and breakdown of earlier treaties; old tensions flaring up between increasingly imperialist powers; and expansionist policies in the Balkans causing tension on all sides.

The actual spark of war was the assassination of Archduke Franz Ferdinand of Austria on 28 June 1914 by Serb nationalists. This led to violence in Bosnia and Herzegovina, ruled by the Austro-Hungarian Empire. One thing led to another and soon the Austro-Hungarian Empire declared war on Serbia;

due to interlocking and complex treaties, all Europe was rapidly drawn into conflict.

Who was involved? France, UK, Russia, Italy, USA, Romania, Japan, Serbia, Belgium and Greece on one side as the Allies (a total of 42 million men under arms). And Germany, the Austro-Hungarian Empire, the Ottoman Empire and Bulgaria on the other as the Central Powers (a total of 25 million men under arms).

Market Place, Derby, 1905. Looking south at the west side of the Market Place, the Victorian Guildhall is just out of view on the left of the photograph. Note the horse-drawn trams on the road. (© 2004 Derby Museums collection DMAG001200)

By the end of the conflict, 5.5 million Allied men had been killed, 12.8 million were wounded and another 4.1 million missing: a total of 22.4 million casualties. Of the Central Powers, 4.3 million men were killed, 8.3 million wounded and 3.6 million missing: a total of 16.4 million casualties. Taking into account the effect on families, loved ones and future generations, that is a staggering 38.8 million lives lost or changed forever.

Derby was settled by both the Romans and the Vikings and is the capital city of the county of Derbyshire, receiving city status in 1977. It is famous for its eighteenth-century Enlightenment legacy (its 1720s silk mill claims to be the first mechanised factory

in the world) and huge output during the Industrial Revolution of the nineteenth century. Today the city hosts Rolls-Royce PLC, which makes half the world's aircraft engines in Derby, and the rail vehicles production facility for Bombardier Inc., which took over the Midland Railway legacy and is now the sole manufacturer of trains in the UK. Derby is one of the few remaining UK cities to export heavy industry products around the world to an extent that affects world economies.

Dr Mike Galer, 2014

1

OUTBREAK OF WAR

Pre-war Derby

The best view of pre-war Derby comes from the 1911 census, from which we can build a picture of what life was like just three years before the war. Comparison with the next census (1921) reveals some interesting changes and some areas where life appears no different, despite the war. The 1911 census was the first where the 'Return' for a household or institution was written directly by the 'Head of Household'. It also asked more detailed questions about employment and industries in which respondents worked, and questions about marriage and children. The census looked at Derby in two ways: just the parliamentary borough (known as Derby PB), which had a population of 105,912 in 1901 and 109,864 in 1911, and the slightly wider context of the county borough of Derby (referred to as Derby CB), which had a population of 114,848 in 1911 and 123,410 in 1911. The 'Derby CB' context is the more widely used throughout the census, and so this book will use that definition throughout. At the time, Alvaston (population 1,398) and a few other areas which we take for granted as belonging to the modern city were considered separate from Derby CB and information was collected separately.

The population of the county borough of Derby in 1901 was 114,848. By 1911, this had grown to 123,410 (59,999 men and 63,411 women), organised in 27,720 families. From 1 April 1901 to 31 March 1911, there were 9,747 marriages, 31,949 births and 17,730 deaths, resulting in an excess of births over deaths of +14,219. Total growth since 1901: +8,562.

The most populated areas of the town were Pear Tree, Normanton, Dale and Abbey wards, each having a population of just under 10,000. Normanton barracks is recorded separately, with 198 'officers and men' recorded and an additional sixteen males and forty-eight females under the 'other inmates' section (presumably servants and washerwomen). Interestingly, forty-one males and twenty-six females are recorded as living 'in the open' or in sheds, barns, tents and caravans. Whether or not these persons would be classed as 'homeless' or 'sleeping rough' (as we might call it today), or just living permanently in very poor housing, is unclear.

The census starts by looking at age, births and marriage and from these we can get a view of a rapidly growing town where births considerably outstrip deaths, but also where people are leaving to go elsewhere as the town's total population is growing at about half the excess of births over deaths. It was a young population; the majority (72 per cent) were aged less than 40, and 60 per cent were unmarried. Very few people were married under the age of 20 in 1911. In fact, only sixty-six people in the whole of Derby were married that young. That said, there was a widower aged just 17 and a 19-year-old widow, revealing the

Cornmarket, Derby 1910s, showing the tower of All Saint's church in the middle. On the left is the statue of Michael Thomas Bass, MP and benefactor to Derby, now moved to Museum Square. (© 2004 Derby Museums collection DMAG000319)

11

harsh realities of life in the early twentieth century. The vast majority of people who were married were aged between 25 and 50; not very different from today.

The census looks at the occupation of males and females in great detail, recording details at an administrative county level (essentially Derbyshire) as well as the county borough of Derby (effectively just the town). Perhaps shocking is that the employment statistics count anyone over the age of 10 as the boundary between a child and a working person; what we might call 'available for work'. Employment among men was quite high: out of those 'available for work', 84 per cent appeared to be employed. Perhaps 16 per cent unemployment sounds high to us today in a political world dominated by various economic indicators, but this includes persons who were classed as 'retired', with their own income (a rare occurrence in 1911), and also, presumably, young persons over the age of 10, but not yet what we call an adult. For women the picture was very different; only 31 per cent were classed as employed, and the rest retired or 'unoccupied', though it is pretty clear that most of these must have been housewives and would likely be unhappy with the term 'unoccupied'. These proportions are largely unchanged in the census of 1921, despite advances in acknowledging women's potential to work.

Looking at women first, what is immediately clear is that there were certain careers and jobs in which there were few, if any, women engaged; shocking to our modern notions of equality. For example, in 1911, there were no female police officers, military personnel, priests or solicitors (though there was one female law clerk in Derby, against ninety-one men and one barrister in 1921). There were four doctors; however, all were unmarried and that number pales in comparison to sixty-one men (although the number of female doctors rose to twelve in 1921). There does, however, appear to have been a fair number of women working in local and national government, most of whom were unmarried. Though it is unclear, these might be secretaries

In 1911, 59,771 people were aged under 25 (13,174 of whom were under 5) and 89,979 were aged under 40. 109 people were aged 85–90, 17 people were aged 90–95 and there were none over the age 95. There were 47,286 males, and 50,591 females were aged over 10. The census records 68,723 unmarried persons, 48,293 married and 6,394 widowed.

or clerks. Perhaps not surprising for the age, quite a number of women were recorded as teachers, nurses, midwives, washerwomen and in the arts. However, the vast majority of those women working are either in domestic service (against very few men) or in textile factories (nearly double the number of men), or associated trades like dressmakers, milliners and similar. A few are recorded in insurance and a large number (but still less than half that of men) in 'commercial occupations'.

In 1911, 39,857 men were employed (7,429 were retired or unoccupied, of which 1,427 received a pension) and 15,678 women were employed (35,018 were retired or unoccupied, of which 147 received a pension and 22,507 were married). Additionally, 75 men are recorded as having 'private means', against 520 women saying the same.

For men, the picture is very different. As indicated above, the professions such as clergy, police, law and medicine are all well represented, but in small numbers overall. Large numbers of men worked on the railways; in engineering and metal work, such as foundries; manufacturing; and in construction, which is understandable given the heavy industry for which Derby was famous. Despite the presence of historical famous ceramic works, relatively few men (and less than half the number of women) appear to have worked in the pottery industries.

Victoria Street, Derby, looking towards St Peter's Street. Published by Philco, series no. 2536. Postmarked 30 March 1912. (© 2013 Derby Museums collection 1984-187/5)

CHILDREN AND YOUNG ADULTS IN WORK IN 1911

According to the 1911 census, there were 5,914 males under 14 (3,666 of them between the ages of 10 and 13) and 5,388 aged between 15 and 20. There were 5,830 females under 14 (3,516 of them between 10 and 13) and 6,058 aged between 15 and 20. These figures reveal a young, growing population, with roughly equal male and female populations.

There were three girls aged between 10 and 13 in work in the whole of Derby, against nineteen boys. Fifty-nine girls aged between 13 and 14 were in work compared to eighty-four boys and 645 girls aged 14 to 15 against 760 boys. Approximately 92 per cent of all boys aged 16 to 17 were in work and 96 per cent of all 'boys' aged 18 to 19 were in some sort of employment. Most of these were working on the railways or in textiles manufactories, but many were in the food and tobacco trades, most likely as delivery boys. The highest number of boys in Derby (between 15 and 16 years old) for any occupation is in the category of 'messengers, porters and watchmen', in which 141 boys were employed, compared to just two girls of the same age.

Records show that 78 per cent of all girls aged 16 to 17 were in work and 81 per cent of all girls aged between 18 and 19 were in some sort of employment; significantly higher than for adult women (31 per cent). For girls and young women, the main occupations were roughly the same as their older counterparts (namely textile manufacturing and domestic service); the highest number of young women in any occupation is recorded against the 'domestic indoor service' category.

Most boys and young men (over 90 per cent) were in some sort of employment, over double the percentage of adult women. What the census does not reveal is the hours worked – which were likely to be long– or their (presumably low) wages.

Cope and Taylor Chemists around 1900. Many young people worked in shops or as delivery boys and girls in establishments like this. © 2004 Derby Museums collection DMAG000013.

Unlike today's Derby, the town does not appear to have been very diverse, with the overwhelming majority of people having been born in Derbyshire, Leicestershire, Staffordshire or Nottinghamshire. The census didn't quite ask the right questions either – the early twentieth century having no real modern understanding of ethnicity – and instead simply asked the question 'where were you born?', rather than questions about ethnicity or nationality of parents that are found in recent censuses. It does make the distinction, however, about whether persons are now 'British Subjects' or 'Naturalised British Subjects'; the rest, rather bluntly, are called 'Foreigners'. Only just fewer than 350 people living in Derby in 1911 were born overseas (seventeen at sea), and those were mainly from Europe, with most people born in France and Germany, followed by Poland and Russia, with a few from Italy. Two residents are recorded as coming from China, one from Japan and two from Africa (both of whom are described as 'British Subjects', so they are likely to be white British). Quite a few people hailed from the USA (110), though all but six were 'British Subjects'. In all, only 160 people in Derby were 'Foreigners' and the highest number (thirty-three) – unfortunately for them, considering what was about to happen – were German.

Victoria Street, Derby, looking towards the Wardwick and Derby Museum and Art Gallery/Library. (© 2013 Derby Museums collection 1988-330/30)

The census also collected information on disabilities at a county level, most under headings likely to cause offence today, namely: totally blind, totally deaf, deaf and dumb, lunatic, imbecile, feeble-minded and combined infirmities with different combinations. Across the county, nearly 2,000 people were entered into the rather vague and likely imprecise mental illness/disability categories (a roughly equal number for men and women) and several hundred for the other categories, again roughly equal for men and women. Information about physical disabilities such as missing limbs, or illnesses likely to cause mobility problems and similar effects, were not recorded in this census.

One other area in which the census attempted to make sense of a complicated state of affairs was the type and quality of housing people occupied. The census analysed the data by looking at the number of rooms per 'tenement' or housing unit and how many people, especially children, lived within. The vast majority of people lived in housing with five or six rooms (just over 80,000 people), with the majority at least having between three and five people per household, but a large number still lived in tenements with four rooms or fewer (nearly 22,000 people in 6,000 families), with the majority of those having between two and four people per household. There was a significant number of families in Derby that had over six people in the family; some were recorded as having as many as between ten and fourteen per family unit, and some of those were living in housing with five rooms or fewer. The statistics are very detailed; for example, eight families comprised eleven people in total and lived in a tenement with fewer than four rooms.

Ordinary Lives and Concerns in 1914 Derby

1914 started quite ordinarily for the people of Derby. Industry was booming, particularly in the metal production trades and machinery manufactories. A new glass bottle-making firm had been attracted to the town and demand for sugar-refining machinery was up. In the early part of the year, a number of

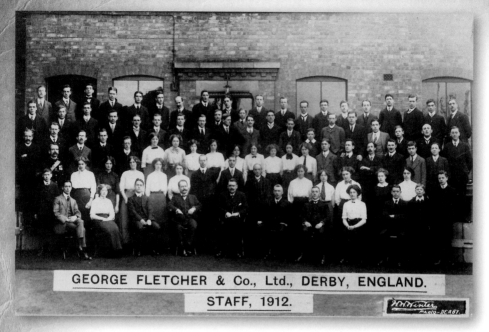

GEORGE FLETCHER & Co., Ltd., DERBY, ENGLAND.

STAFF, 1912.

The staff of George Fletcher and Co., 1912, who made sugar-refining machines for the West Indies. (© 2013 Derby Museums collection 1985-286/431)

serious fires threatened the town, with a number of businesses affected; for example, in March, a motor-car facility in Bourne Street burnt impressively, drawing large crowds, and in May, the mills of Thomas Smith & Son in Abbey Street were seriously damaged by fire (the spate of fires was covered by the *Derby Daily Telegraph*). There was also industrial action, with a strike at Leys Malleable Castings Co., which occurred after the management sacked a number of men. There were labour difficulties at Rolls-Royce too in June and July, forcing the company to declare that they were in talks with unions and denying that they had dismissed lots of men, but stating it was unlikely that many of its European orders for luxury cars would be fulfilled, and that they might have to move to a war footing soon.

The famous socialist leader Keir Hardie addressed the local Derby branch of the Independent Labour Party at the Temperance Hall in February, where he had not talked since 1894. Suffragette meetings were also held at the Temperance Hall in February, March (with Mrs Pethick-Lawrence as principle speaker) and in June at the Market Place, where Mrs Pethick-Lawrence denied that they were anti-men or anti-Liberal.

Some of these meetings, particularly open-air events in Breadsall, were said to have an air of menace about them. 'Vote for Women' messages were found scrawled at the premises of Mr Sowter's millinery shop at The Spot after a window was broken in May. A fire which nearly destroyed Breadsall church on 5 June 1914 was blamed on the suffragettes, based on an open window, a hat-pin and a posted message hinting (but not quite claiming) responsibility.

There were balls held in February at the Assembly Rooms for the Meynell Hunt for the leading families of Staffordshire and Derbyshire, and at the Drill Hall (Royal Drill Hall, Beckett Street, the headquarters of the 5th Battalion Sherwood Foresters) for the annual Midland Railway Ball. The Drill Hall was transformed with bright lights and people were provided with free rail and omnibus travel from the station. April was considered to be one of the hottest months, with brilliant weather, although at least one child died of heat exhaustion. In July, also in fine weather, the annual mayor's Garden Party was held at Garfield House, Littleover, with over 700 people attending, according to the *Derby Daily Telegraph*.

> Top occupations: 4,755 men and 13 women worked on 'The Railways'. An additional 2,141 were employed in making coaches and wagons (7 of them women). There were 7,697 men (and 97 women) in heavy industry and a further 588 (91 women) in electrical engineering. 1,472 men and 3,481 women worked in in textile manufacturing. Meanwhile, 2,641 women worked in indoor domestic service (as well as 33 men).

Postcard of Market Place, Derby, c. 1905. (© 2013 Derby Museums collection 1988-330/31)

Elsewhere, there were park-band concerts in June at the arboretum (among other venues), and the Derby Sketching Club held its 27th exhibition at the Athenaeum Room in February, featuring A.J. Keene's watercolours and works by Ernest Townsend. At the museum and art gallery, there was an exhibition focusing on embroidery, including items by William Morris and Edward Burne-Jones.

Midland Railway Station, Midland Road, c. 1910. (© 2004 Derby Museums collection DMAG001068)

The platform of Midland Railway Station, Midland Road, c. 1910. (© 2004 Derby Museums collection DMAG001065)

In early May, in fields and above streets near the Nottingham Road cemetery, large crowds enjoyed an air display by flyer Gustav Hamel, who looped the loop several times. Hamel, who was born in 1889, went missing on 23 May 1914, shortly after this display, while returning from Paris in a monoplane he had just collected. In June – according to the *Derby Daily Telegraph* – a statue dedicated to Florence Nightingale was unveiled by the Duke of Devonshire in London Road.

The Derby Royal Hospital, meanwhile, celebrated a new wing for 'consumptives', opened in April by Dr Laurie, and there was a new tuberculosis dispensary in St Helen's Street.

A postcard from Derby, showing London Road and the Florence Nightingale statue. It was sent to F. Hainsworth of the Derbyshire Yeomanry while serving in Salonika, May 1916. (© 2013 Derby Museums collection 2004-827/15)

The Calm before the Storm

An examination of the newspapers just before the war in July 1914 reveals a chillingly ordinary calm, with little sign of the war that was about to engulf the world. The articles and news are all about local matters, sports, marriages and death notices, councilmen arguing with each other, crime, the general minutiae of local communities and the weather. The *Derby Daily Telegraph* in particular has many advertisements which set the tone for what was ordinary life in Derby in the pre-war period, many of which looked to the future with optimism, such as the advert for 'Summer Holidays' from the Great Western Railway (known as 'The Holiday Line') throughout June 1914, which offers holidays in Cornwall: 'If this year's holiday is to be an ideal one, spend it in the beautiful Cornish Rivera; pre-eminent as a holiday ground for tourists, artists, sportsmen and health-seekers alike.'

There are very few signs of the brewing trouble in Europe. Buried deep in the regimental notices of the *Derby Mercury* there are glimpses of ordinary military life: Lieutenant Colonel Lord Cavendish-Bentinck of the Derbyshire Yeomanry orders all permanent staff Squadron Sergeant Majors to report by 11 July 1914 and instructs them to collect 'the whole of the British warm coats of the NCOs and men of their squadrons, and forward same to headquarters by the 18th inst'. There is also a detailed notice from the 4th North Midland (Howitzer) Brigade RFA (Derbyshire Artillery) about training, lectures, benefits and other small matters, but nothing to suggest actual war. By 31 July, however, the regimental notices columns were growing in size and detail, suggesting a great interest in mobilisation, with

Lithograph of Kedleston Road, Derby, postmarked 12 July 1906. (© 2013 Derby Museums collection 1984-285/2)

detailed accounts of various procedures and lots of details regarding the Sherwood Foresters Territorial Force battalions' annual training which, in 1914, was at Filey. Incidentally, this training ended early and on the day before the declaration of war, the Sherwood Foresters volunteers marched through the town on their return from the Midland Station to the Drill Hall, to the reception of enthusiastic crowds.

This is not to say there was nothing in the 'civilian' sections about war and the military, but it was theoretical rather than actual; for example, an interesting article in the *Derby Mercury* on 10 July 1914 entitled 'Steerable Balloons and Aeroplanes, the progress in 1914' looked at the military potential of these devices and suggested France was the current leader in numbers of trained pilots and technology of planes, but warned of rapid German development and the quality of their factories, hinting that though not 'elegant', they were 'more robust and more reliable' than other nations.

The *Derby Mercury* does – rather unsurprisingly – cover in detail the royal visit of King George V and Queen Mary on 2 July 1914 to Ilkeston and Heanor, where the 5th Battalion Sherwood Foresters, the Lads Brigade and the Boy Scouts, along with 8,000 schoolchildren, lined the streets: 'not a single building was without flags and other decorations.' The newspaper goes on to explain that the great and the good of the area were there; shops sold space outside their frontages to small stallholders; and that many songs were sung, including the national anthem, 'Hearts of Oak', 'Here's Health unto His Majesty', 'Land of Hope and Glory', 'John Peel' and 'Rule, Britannia!'. This one event, in some respects, sums up the age and how nationalism and patriotism were tied together with honour, love and respect for the Royal Family and their representation of the British Empire.

War!

Then, on 5 August 1914, war was declared and the *Derby Daily Telegraph* ran the following headlines: 'Great Britain and Germany – British Ultimatum on Belgian Neutrality' and, on the same page, 'Violation of Belgian Neutrality: Germans Cross the Frontier: The British Government has received official information from the Belgian Government that the German Forces have crossed to Belgian Soil', then, finally, 'Britain at War with Germany: Europe faced with a life and death struggle'. Suddenly all pretence of normality was over and the newspaper provided details of the declaration of war; immediate actions (for example news of the sinking of a British ship by the Germans, men killed in a pit explosion and the dismantling of radio stations in Derbyshire) and evocative sub-headlines like 'wild scenes in London' and notices informing people of the immediate increase in bread prices. It was all quite negative and salacious with a hint of hysteria, and not like the stiff-upper-lip and gentle Edwardian resolve that you might have expected. This was the first day, however: things rapidly calmed down and the business of winning the war soon began.

Switching to the *Derby Mercury* of 7 August 1914, reportage became more modest and dignified. The headlines were tough and hard-hitting, but there was an air of resolve and duty; furthermore, any news of German activity was almost entirely negative and couched in terms of their incompetence.

Most of the articles were not about local events and people, but of national importance. Much of the phraseology was

The Derby Daily Telegraph *headline announcing the outbreak of war, 5 August 1914. (© 2014 Derby Telegraph)*

BRITAIN AT WAR WITH GERMANY.
EMPIRE FACED WITH A LIFE AND DEATH STRUGGLE.

patriotic in the extreme and concentrated on British and Allied success and German failure; the business of winning the war with words had begun. 'German Losses – Army Routed in Belgium'; 'Opening of Naval Warfare – German mine-layer sunk by British Cruiser'; 'The German Rout – brilliant success of the Belgian Army', who – contrary to historical fact – were apparently 'victorious' and also 'brilliant'; 'Belgian forces drive back German invaders'; and, finally, quite calmly and matter-of-factly, 'England at War, Hostilities with Germany Begun'.

Friday 14 August was more of the same: 'England at War with Austria', explaining in detail the official announcement to 'begin hostilities' and the reasons for war. Perhaps typically for a local paper, the front page was also concerned with the announcement that the Derbyshire Association of Football had decided to carry on, giving this equal space. Amongst this were the usual adverts, including one from Horniman's Tea, proudly announcing: 'The War: No increase in the price of Horniman's Tea.'

In the 7 August 1914 edition of the newspaper, there were a number of special articles of a more local nature and some provided practical advice (as well as propagandist words of wisdom). For example, there was an announcement that the Duke of Devonshire had placed the ground floor of Devonshire House, London, at 'the disposal of the British Red Cross' and so the notion of sacrifice and duty began in earnest, starting with those at the very top of British society. Later in August came a further announcement: 'Derbyshire and The War – Relief fund opened', remarking on the duke's efforts to create a Derbyshire fund to help relieve 'distress in time of war'.

An article entitled 'How to be useful in War time' (apparently copied from *The Times* by the local press) provides useful advice and, from our point of view, a very illuminating insight into the mindset of the time. 'First and foremost, keep your heads. Be calm. Go about your ordinary business quietly and soberly. Do not indulge in excitement or foolish demonstrations. Secondly, think of others more than you are wont to do. Think of your duty to your neighbour. Think of the common weal.'

Citizens were also advised, 'do not hoard gold' and 'pay what you owe especially… [to] washwomen and charwomen'. And finally, 'do what you can to cheer and encourage our soldiers. Gladly help any organisation for their comfort and welfare. Explain to the young and the ignorant what war is, and why we have been forced to wage it.' It is interesting to note that, as far as the newspapers saw it, Britain had been 'forced' into the war and seemingly had no choice in the matter; nevertheless, people must do their duty regardless.

There was also an account of Sir Alfred Haslam's (Mayor of Derby 1890–91) experiences in Germany (detailed in the *Derby Mercury* on 28 August 1914). He had been caught out in Germany at the outset of war before being detained briefly in Homburg. He got home safely soon enough ('Sir Alfred Haslam Safe', *Derby Daily Telegraph*, 19 August 1914). His son, Captain William Kenneth Seale Haslam, was killed in action in France on 27 March 1917 while serving with 4th (North Midland) Brigade, RFA. His other son, Captain Eric Seale Haslam, was an officer in the same artillery unit from 1913, but survived the war.

By 28 August, there were accounts of actual fighting, such as a report of the action at Mons under the headline of 'How the British fought – deadly marksmanship of the infantry'. However, the accounts (passed by the press bureau) are clearly propaganda and emphasise the derring-do of the British soldiers: '…our cavalrymen charged the much-valued German horsemen as the Berserks of old might have done.' (*Derby Mercury*, 28 August 1914).

Considering how early in the war this was, these editions of the *Derby Mercury* were full of small articles concerning the real and practical considerations of what war meant on this scale. It is often assumed that the general public at this time were naïve and ill-informed; unwittingly allowing themselves to be dragged into a horrific war. There is no doubt that there are signs of this, but the articles reveal that the public were preparing themselves for war and, more importantly, preparing to help. The best example of both naïvety and realism can be found in the article 'Wounds in Battle – how modern arms injure', which provides a gruesome account of how weapons wound and injure, though curiously not how they kill. Chillingly, even mutilations are mentioned in a cheery kind of fashion, perhaps in an attempt at optimism. What is striking is how the author declares that bayonet charges and lance charges are a thing of the past and that modern cartridges have reduced the suffering of the wounded. He would be proven wrong on both counts.

2

PREPARATIONS AT HOME

Defence of the Realm Act (DORA)

The Defence of the Realm Act (DORA) was passed in the early weeks of 1914 and it governed all aspects of normal life in Britain during the First World War. Its original intention was to prepare the country for possible invasion and to keep up morale, imposing restrictions on the press and on ordinary people for speaking negatively about the war and other matters. DORA was added to as the war progressed and it listed everything that people were not allowed to do in time of war. Later versions included general public safety powers; emergency powers for the government to take over land, buildings and factories; and included clauses intended to prevent spying and passing of information to the enemy. Ultimately, the Act was used to intro-duce rationing in 1918 (*see* Chapter 5).

Some of the restrictions might sound strange to us now, but many had practical intentions and real outcomes, and make sense when considered in the context of the war. Some of the banned activities included: talking about naval or military matters in public places, or spreading rumours about military matters; buying binoculars or melting down gold or silver; lighting bonfires or fireworks; giving bread to horses or chickens; using invisible ink when writing abroad; buying brandy or whisky in a railway refreshment room; ringing church bells. As the war continued and evolved, the government introduced more clauses

National Registration Act 1915 identity cards for Mr and Mrs Morgan of 262 Uttoxeter Road, Derby. (© 2013 Derby Museums collection 1990-44/10)

to DORA, including introducing 'British Summer Time' to give more daylight for extra work and cutting pub opening hours, as well as watering down beer and, perhaps rather oddly, banning the purchase of a round of drinks.

In fact, there was a whole range of legislation that was enacted during the war which gave special powers to the government and controlled a number of different issues. These included the National Registration Act 1915, which provided for a register of all persons between the ages of 15 and 65 who were not members of the armed forces. The information supplied under the Act provided manpower statistics and also enabled the military authorities to discriminate between persons who should be called up for military service and those who should, in the national interest, be retained in civil employment. It required people to have an Identity Card which listed your name, address and occupation.

Other Acts of this period included the Military Service Act 1916 (which introduced conscription), Trading with the Enemy Act 1914 (which prevented trading with persons of 'an enemy character') and the Munitions of War Act 1915 (which brought private companies supplying the armed forces under the tight control of the newly created Ministry of Munitions, regulating wages, hours and employment conditions), among many others.

Enlistment and Recruitment

At the outset of the war, Britain sent the bulk of the Regular Army to France as the British Expeditionary Force (BEF), which included units of the Regular Army and some of the Territorial Force. Kaiser Wilhelm II, the Emperor of Germany, had reportedly referred to the BEF as a 'contemptible little army' and given orders to exterminate it, though no evidence of any such order being issued by the kaiser has ever been found and may therefore have been a British propaganda invention, and one often repeated as fact. Nevertheless, whether fact or fiction, as a result, the survivors of the Regular Army dubbed themselves 'The Old Contemptibles' to distinguish themselves from later volunteers and conscripts. The BEF consisted of six infantry divisions and five cavalry brigades that were arranged into the I Corps and the II Corps. In October 1914, the 7th Division arrived in France, forming the basis of the III Corps, by which point the cavalry had grown to form the Cavalry Corps of the three divisions. By December 1914, the BEF had expanded and had been reorganised into the First Army and the Second Army. By the end of 1914, after the battles of Mons, Le Cateau, the Aisne and Ypres, the old Regular Army had suffered massive casualties and had been wiped out as an effective fighting force, but had managed to stop the German advance.

On the same day as the declaration of war (5 August 1914), the *Derby Daily Telegraph* printed an article calling for men to enlist (*see* image opposite).It was strong stuff indeed, and one that was answered by young men everywhere.

The *Derby Mercury* in August carried several articles regarding recruitment and enlistment, including the mobilisation of the existing Territorial Force Derby and Derbyshire units, under the headings: 'The Call to Duty' and 'Concentration of Troops in Derby'. The newspaper announced that 'practically the whole' of the units comprising the North Midlands (NM) Brigade were stationed in or near the town by 14 August. The NM Brigade was comprised of the 5th Battalion, Sherwood Foresters, the 4th NM Howitzer Brigade, the 1st NM Field

Ambulance and the whole of the Derbyshire Yeomanry. They were soon joined in Derby by the 6th, 7th and 8th Battalions of the Sherwood Foresters (from Chesterfield, Nottingham and Newark respectively), the Northampton Yeomanry, the Notts. & Derby Army Service Corps and the local Territorial units of the Royal Engineers. Soon, this 'Citizen Army', as it was called by the newspaper, numbered around 9,000 to 10,000 soldiers and was billeted around the town in schools, public halls and private houses. The senior staff and officers were billeted at the Town Hall and elsewhere around the town. In Belper, the Lincoln and Leicester Infantry had gathered, along with the Lincoln and Leicester Army Service Corps and the 2nd NM Field Ambulance and in Borrowash, the 1st Brigade of the Royal Field Artillery had assembled.

The newspapers of the time detail explicitly the terms of how people put up these billeted soldiers, under an article entitled 'Billeting Terms – The Daily Dietary of the Soldiers', which explained what food should be given and the amount in compensation the provider would get in return from the government:

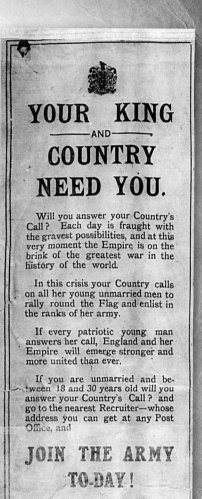

The Derby Daily Telegraph *recruitment notice:* 'Your King and Country Need You', *5 August 1914. (© 2014* Derby Evening Telegraph)

Lodging and breakfast, attendance for soldier 9*d* a night; six ounces of bread, 1 pint of tea with milk and sugar and 4 ounces of bacon for breakfast, 7½*d* each man. Dinner; (hot) I pound of meat, 8 ounces of bread, 8 ounces of potatoes or other vegetables. 1 pint of beer or mineral water, 1s [shilling] 7½*d*. Supper; 6 ounces of bread, 1 pint of tea with milk and sugar and 2 ounces of cheese, 4½*d*.

Officers being billeted were also compensated for at a rate of 3*s* a night, but had to pay the provider for their own food.

The *Derby Mercury* also talks of recruiting for 'Kitchener's 2nd Army' (named after Lord H. Kitchener, the Secretary of State for War) and the work by the Duke of Devonshire as president of the Derbyshire Territorial Association, working with the 'local authorities' to open two registers: one for single men aged between 19 and 30 who were willing to serve in the Regular Army, and the other for those between 17 and 35 years of age, who would join the Territorial Force for one year, or the period of the war. In this period there are lots of appeals for and accounts of recruiting, which were held in school halls in Ashbourne, Barrow-on-Trent, Littleover, Borrowash and Ockbrook and Normanton and Darley Abbey, to name a few, to discuss and create these registers of names.

By early 1915, the strength of the Regular Army had been replaced by the part-time volunteers of the Territorial Force (who were, for the most part, already signed on as 'weekend' soldiers or reservists from previous Regular Army service) and early recruits from Kitchener's new volunteer army (following the famous poster campaign of a stern-looking moustached Kitchener pointing his finger with the text, 'Britons: [Kitchener] wants you. Join Your Country's Army. God Save The King'). A well-known feature of this era and the early volunteer army was the Pals

1979 view of Normanton Barracks, which were built in 1874–77 and closed in 1963. Today, the site is occupied by the Showcase Cinema and the Oast House Pub. (© 2004 Derby Museums collection DMAG002072)

battalions (an idea often credited to Lord Derby of Liverpool, who referred to a 'battalion of pals'), often recruited from single communities, villages, companies and factories, who were allowed to serve together.

As far as it is known, no actual 'Pals battalion' was formed specifically in Derby with that in mind or using that term. The majority of known 'Pals Battalions' came from Liverpool, Newcastle, Glasgow, Leeds, Durham, Salford, the Football Association and some of the public schools. This doesn't mean that there were no similar battalions formed in Derby, however. For example, the 16th (Service) Battalion (Chatsworth Rifles) of the Sherwood Foresters was formed at Derby on 16 April 1915 by the Duke of Devonshire and the Derbyshire Territorial Force Association and went on to serve in France in 1916 (see the section on pp.37–41 for further detail of the Derby-formed regiments). They were not, however, 'Pals' in the sense that the other cities formed them (for example the Newcastle Railway Pals (17th Battalion, Northumberland Fusiliers)).

The Kitchener recruitment campaign had proved to be very successful, as on 1 September 1914, over 30,000 men enlisted.

> By the end of September 1914, over 750,000 men had enlisted, increasing to 1 million by January 1915 and 2.25 million by September 1915. In total, almost 2.5 million men volunteered for Kitchener's Army. In 1915, the total available number of men of military age was 5.5 million (with 500,000 more reaching the age each year).

Officers and men of 5th Battalion Notts. & Derby, leaving Derby at a train station in 1914. There has been some debate over the years where exactly this is, but it has been suggested that the image shows Pear Tree station. (© 2004 Derby Museums collection DMAG002071)

Two young recruits— most likely brothers – of the Sherwood Foresters, standing next to a younger sibling too young to join, but obviously proud of his brothers. It is likely that he in turn would have eventually signed up or would have been conscripted. This image was taken taken around 1914. (© 2013 Derby Museums collection 1986-281/5.1)

NOTICE.

The WAR OFFICE has COMMANDEERED

most of our Horses and all our Motor Vehicles.

We are glad to be of service to the State.

We expect to be able to execute all orders entrusted to us.

Should there be some little delay during the next few days we crave the indulgence of our customers, and hope quickly to be in a position to serve them as promptly as heretofore.

STRETTONS DERBY BREWERY, Ltd.,

Brewers & Wine & Spirit Merchants,

ASHBOURNE ROAD, DERBY.

Telephone Numbers, 587 and 588.   Telegrams, Strettons, Derby.

An advert from Stretton's Derby Brewery Ltd, advising that all their horses had been commandeered and that service would be affected for a few days, 6 August 1914. (© 2014 Derby Evening Telegraph)

The British Government soon realised the drawbacks of this system: men with possible vital skills were allowed to leave factories and companies, damaging the war effort, and, on a more sinister note, entire communities could be wiped out and killed in one action or battle, with huge implications for morale back home.

Kitchener's armies were known as 'Ks', and split into 'Army Groups' with a number – K1, K2, K3 and so on – made up of a number of divisions (usually six). Each division was split into three brigades of infantry, mounted troops, artillery and support forces, such as engineers, pioneers, signalers and medical personnel. Those recruited into the New Army were used to form complete battalions under existing British Army regiments. The first (volunteer) New Army divisions were used at the Battle of Loos in the

By 1917, the number of healthy recruits was declining. In 1917–18, 36 per cent of men examined were suitable for full military duties, while 40 per cent were totally unfit or were classified as unable to undergo physical exertion. In 1918, the army was smaller than in 1917 and almost half the infantry was 19 or younger.

The total number of troops and equipment in an army division was as follows:

Men: 19,614
Horses and mules: 5,818
Guns: 48 x 18 pounder, 16 x 4.5in howitzer, 4 x 60 pounder; 52 Vickers machine guns
Assorted carts & vehicles: 958
Cycles: 538
Motorcycles: 19
Cars: 11
Lorries: 4
Ambulances: 21

autumn of 1915, and later at the Battle of the Somme. The rest of Kitchener's armies and those with conscripts saw service later in 1916.

With falling numbers of volunteers in 1915, the government was forced to look at other options to make up the numbers. The National Registration Act in 1915 created a register that revealed the number of men still available (and who had avoided enlistment), and they were targeted in a number of clever and subtle ways, using propaganda and guilt tactics. The skills and techniques of product advertising were used with posters, public meetings and speeches, tales of German atrocities, and the threat of shame: 'Women of Britain, say "GO".' The 'Derby Scheme' (Lord Derby's idea) used door-to-door visits to gather men to 'attest' to serve, if needed, with a promise that bachelors would be called up before married men. The Military Service Bill was enacted with effect from January 1916 and specified that men from the ages of 18 to 41 were liable to be called up for service unless they were married (or widowed with children), or else served in one of a number of reserved professions (see Chapter 3). By the end of the war, almost a quarter of the total male population of the United Kingdom had joined up, totalling over 5 million men.

Derby and Derbyshire Military Units and Military Establishments in Derby

There were a number of pre-existing 'Territorial Force' (TF) units and volunteer battalions serving in Derby and Derbyshire that were not part of the Regular Army and who were immediately activated and mobilised on the outbreak of war. These were:

- 5th Battalion Sherwood Foresters (later called 1st/5th), Notts. & Derby and 1st Volunteer Battalion Sherwood Foresters (Derbyshire Regiment) A, B, C, D, H, I, K Companies. Headquarters section (plus A, B, C and D Companies), based at Royal Drill Hall, Becket Street (the Drill Hall Vaults are the only remains of this now).

- 4th North Midland (Howitzer) Brigade, Royal Field Artillery (RFA) (Derbyshire Artillery). Made up of 1st and 2nd Derbyshire (Howitzer) Battery, 4th Midland (Howitzer) Ammunition Column, whose headquarters were at 91 Siddals Road (long since demolished).

- 1st North Midland Field Ambulance, Royal Army Medical Corp (RAMC) – part of the 46th (North Midland) Division. Made up of A, B and C Sections and, in 1912, 1st North Midland Mounted Brigade Field Ambulance, Royal Army Medical Corps. They were based at St Mary's Gate.

Part of the North Midland Division, Royal Field Artillery (RFA) on the move near Derby. (© 2013 Derby Museums collection 1989-520/2)

- The Derbyshire Yeomanry. C & D Squadrons headquartered at 91 Siddals Road.

New units were quickly formed – mostly additional battalions added to the Sherwood Foresters – as follows:

- 1/6th Battalion, raised in August 1914 in Chesterfield; 1/7th (Robin Hood) Battalion, raised in August 1914 in Nottingham; 1/8th Battalion, raised in August 1914 in Newark. Along with the 1/5th served with the 139th Brigade in 46th (North Midland) Division. Later joined by 2/8th Battalion, formed at Newark on 11 September 1914 as a second-line unit.

The men of the Royal Field Artillery (RFA), Derbyshire Artillery, somewhere in England. (© 2013 Derby Museums collection 1986-281/4.4)

- 2/5th Battalion, formed at Derby on 16 October 1914; 2/6th Battalion, formed at Chesterfield on 14 September 1914; 2/7th (Robin Hood) Battalion, formed at Nottingham on 19 September 1914, becoming the 176th Brigade, 59th (2nd North Midland) Division in August. Moved to Ireland in April 1916 to quell disturbances. Moved in January 1917 to France.

Postcard of a field ambulance struggling in the mud. The 1st North Midland Field Ambulance, Royal Army Medical Corp (RAMC) was part of 46th (North Midland) Division. (© 2013 Derby Museum Collection, 1979-374/6.2)

A postcard of a group of Derbyshire Yeomanry at camp, believed to be Aldershot, in 1913. Part of a collection of items relating to Private F. Wragg, 1/1st Derbyshire Yeomanry. (© 2013 Derby Museums collection 1989-541/3)

- 3/5th, 3/6th, 3/7th and 3/8th Battalions, formed at home bases in March 1915 and moved to Grantham in October 1915. On 8 April 1916 became 5th, 6th, 7th and 8th Reserve.

The Derbyshire Yeomanry digging at Chatsworth 1912/13. (© 2013 Derby Museums collection 2007-316/40)

Battalions of the New Army (all men volunteers):

- 9th (Service) Battalion, formed at Derby in August 1914 as part of K1 and came under orders of 33rd Brigade in 11th (Northern) Division. Dispatched to Gallipoli, landing at Suvla Bay 7 August 1915. Moved to France in July 1916.

- 10th (Service) Battalion, formed at Derby in September 1914 as part of K2 and came under orders of 51st Brigade in 17th (Northern) Division. Moved to France (Boulogne) on 14 July 1915.

- 11th (Service) Battalion, formed at Derby in September 1914 as part of K3 and came under orders of 70th Brigade in 23rd Division. Landed at Boulogne 27 August 1915. Moved with Division to Italy in November 1917 and back to France in late 1918.

- 12th (Service) Battalion (Pioneers), formed at Derby on 1 October 1914 as part of K3 and attached as army troops to 24th Division. Landed in France 29 August 1915.

- 14th (Reserve) Battalion, formed at Lichfield in October 1914 as a Service battalion for K4 and came under orders of 91st Brigade, originally 30th Division. On 1 September 1916 they converted to 13th Training Reserve Battalion of 3rd Reserve Brigade at Brocton.

- 16th (Service) Battalion (Chatsworth Rifles), formed at Derby on 16 April 1915 by the Duke of Devonshire and the Derbyshire TF Association. Moved to Buxton on 4 May 1915 and then near Sheffield on 8 June. 2 September 1915, came orders of 117th Brigade in 39th Division. Moved to France 1916.

- 18th (Service) Battalion, formed at Derby on 27 July 1915 as a Bantam Battalion. October 1915: moved to Aldershot and came under orders of 121st Brigade in 40th Division. 2 April 1916: absorbed by the 13th Battalion, the Yorkshire Regiment at Woking.

- 20th (Labour) Battalion, formed in Derby in May 1916. June 1916: landed in France, moved to Fifth Army.

- 1st Garrison Battalion, formed at Lichfield in July 1915 and moved in October to Malta and then onto Egypt, where it remained.

THE SHERWOOD FORESTERS

The Sherwood Foresters were formed during the 1881 British Army reforms. It was formed from a merger of the 45th (Nottinghamshire) Regiment of Foot (raised in 1741, the regiment saw action in the American War of Independence, the Napoleonic wars in Europe and the South African campaigns of the 1850s) and the 95th (Derbyshire) Regiment of Foot (raised in 1823, they saw action in the Crimea War of 1854 and the Indian Mutiny of 1857), who were redesignated as the 1st and 2nd battalions of the Sherwood Foresters (Derbyshire Regiment). The Derbyshire and Royal Sherwood Foresters Militias became the 3rd Battalion (Robin Hood Rifles) and 4th Battalion respectively. These were joined by the 1st and 2nd (Derbyshire) and the 3rd and 4th (Nottinghamshire) volunteer battalions. The headquarters of the regimental district was established at Derby at Normanton Barracks.

The Sherwood Foresters saw action in Egypt in 1882, as part of the Anglo-Egyptian War between Egyptian and Sudanese forces under Ahmed Orabi; in Tirah, India in 1897–98; and in South Africa during the Boer War (South African War) 1899–1902.

In 1902, the Nottinghamshire association was made explicit and the name was changed to the Sherwood Foresters (Nottingham and Derbyshire) Regiment. By the time of the First World War, the regiment was often known as 'Notts. & Derby' and that phrase is often interchangeable with 'the Sherwood Foresters'. They served throughout the Second World War, with many honours. The Sherwood Foresters merged with the Worcestershire Regiment in 1970 to become the Worcestershire and Sherwood Foresters (or WFR, lending rise to the nickname 'The Woofers'. Since September 2007, the legacy of the Sherwood Foresters continues as 2nd Battalion (light infantry), the Mercian Regiment, serving in Iraq and Afghanistan throughout the 2000s and 2010s.

The Sherwood Foresters (Notts. & Derby A Company) marching at Lulworth training camp around 1914. (© 2013 Derby Museum Collection, 1985-257/1.38)

Home Defence

On 18 December 1914, the Duke of Devonshire chaired a meeting at Derby to determine the steps to be taken in the event of the enemy attempting an invasion. It was decided to co-ordinate all the existing Volunteer Training Corps (for example the Derby Physical Training & Rifle Club, which was formed 10 September 1914 for the purpose of Home Defence) and by the end of January 1915 (inaugurated 25 January 1915), the Derbyshire Regiment of Home Guard had been brought into being, with Colonel H. Brooke-Taylor as the Commanding Officer, and the Duke as the Regimental Adjutant. The regimental headquarters were to be at the Town Hall Chambers, Bakewell, though the headquarters appear to have been moved to Derby by 1916. There were 830 men attached to the Derby Borough Battalion by 31 October 1915, with additional sections based in Buxton, Osmaston-by-Ashbourne, Staveley, Chesterfield, Belper, Ilkeston and Elvaston; a total of 6,413 men. The battalion at Derby was equipped with 200 Victorian-era Martini rifles, twenty-four miniature BSA rifles and a small rifle range erected at a cost of £100 (opened at Beckett Street on 31 May 1915). It is noted in the 'Derbyshire Red Book' that about half the men had purchased their own uniform.

The Derby Home Guard were not idle. In April 1915, they formed a Derby Home Guard Cyclist Corps and, in August, a Motor Transport Section. They conducted a large review of themselves at Buxton in front of their colonel, the Duke of Devonshire, and in November 1915 organised a special route march to Ashbourne and back (which took two days).

Almost like the 'Dad's Army' of the Second World War, the idea was for these volunteer older men, many of whom had seen service in earlier wars (for example the Zulu and Afghanistan wars of the 1870s and in particular the Boer War of 1899–1902), to take up duties of guarding train stations, post offices and the like and to remain vigilant against the risks of invasion. Unlike the Second World War, when there was a much higher risk of air attack, there was not a great deal for them to do. However, the morale and propaganda value of such a Home Guard was very valuable and kept older men and local dignitaries feeling that they were involved and engaged with the war.

Fundraising and War Bonds

Early on in the war, there were a number of local efforts to secure funds for relief of various 'charitable' activities associated with the war, such as aid to wounded soldiers and their families, rather than directly raising money for the government and the war itself. For example, on 12 September 1914 there was a 'Forget-me-not-day', where flowers were sold throughout Derby in aid of the War Relief Fund, and on 16 October 1914, there was a 'service of sacred music' in All Saint's church (the cathedral) in aid of the wounded, sick and aged soldiers and sailors. This must have been an existing charity, as there could not have been many 'aged' veteran soldiers of the First World War at this point. Meanwhile, at the hippodrome on 12 December 1914 there was a Grand Matinee concert for the Belgian Relief Fund (an aid programme for Belgian citizens displaced by the advancing German Army). This continued throughout 1915 and 1916 with similar events, but slowly these were added to with memorial services for the fallen (such as a memorial service at St James' church for 'Derby's Fallen Heroes on the Battlefield' on 19 November 1915), events relating to refugees (Derby Belgian Refugee's

An advert in the Derby Daily Telegraph, 7 November 1918 for war bonds. (© 2014 Derby Evening Telegraph)

The
LORD MAYOR'S
MESSAGE

THE retiring Lord Mayor of London, Sir Charles Hanson, has issued the following inspiring call to action :

"Four years and more have passed since first our guns flung back the insolent challenge of the War Lords.

"The Guns spoke at Jutland—and the High Seas Fleet still shuns the British Navy. They spoke in China, Africa, the Pacific ; and the German Colonial Empire is to-day little more than an evil memory.

"They spoke in Mesopotamia—and Bagdad fell ; in Palestine ; and the Last Crusade has been won. They sounded amid the crests of the Balkans ; Bulgaria heard them and surrendered.

"They echo to-day from the Adriatic to the Alps, with the promise of liberty for peoples long exiled and oppressed. They thunder to-day on the Western Front as our soldiers advance along the road that leads to final victory."

Live to Lend

"What is the message of the guns for us, here in Britain ? They bid us redouble our effort, moral and financial. They claim from us more self-denial ; more resolution ; more of the spirit of patriotic thrift. Each one of us—each man and woman—each City and Town and Village—must be filled, in these historic hours, with a deeper sense of civic responsibility.

"We must *live to lend* our full share of the £25,000,000 required week by week. Our full share is the utmost we can possibly afford. Anything short of that would mean failure in our duty to our country and to the men behind the guns."

FEED THE GUNS
with
WAR BONDS
and help to end the War

Reunion meeting at the Gospel Hall on1 January 1915) and charitable events, such as various Red Cross Flag Days (for example, one was held on 23 October 1915) and examination of the life of the soldier, such as illustrated lectures (one example being the lecture 'How the British Soldier is fighting' by A. Sydney Watson, at the Royal Drill Hall, Derby, in aid of the Belgian Relief Fund on 11 January 1915).

More 'official' war support was available in the form of war bonds and government war loans, where people could 'invest' their money in government bonds, which paid fixed interests. The war was expensive and the government continued to push these right up to the end of the war, as can be seen by articles and advertisements in the November 1918 editions of the *Derby Daily Telegraph*. Sometimes the selling of war bonds was tied to a large event such as 'Derby Gun Week', the last of which was held the week beginning 18 November 1918 and advertised in the 7 November 1918 edition of the *Derby Daily Telegraph* (with

Scene in the Market Place during 'Gun Week', 18–23 November 1918, by Ernest Townsend. (© 2013 Derby Museum Collection, 1936-619/194)

the knowledge that the war might be over). It was a grand affair, with '6 big howitzers' on display with other vehicles, alongside captured German guns. The advert states that the idea was to be as 'realistic as possible … there will be gun drills and gas attacks, the firing of parachutes … in short everything will be done to create the illusion of a battle front – trenches and all the external evidences of warfare as seen on the Western Front'. The main reason, though, was to sell war bonds: '… the people of Derby will not be allowed to forget the part they have played in the war, any more than the part that in the last resource they may still be called on to play in bringing Germany to a

becoming realisation of her guilt.' Sold war bonds and war saving certificates were 'stamped on the guns' in a visual indicator of the number sold.

Derby also took part in raising funds (the *Derby Daily Telegraph* reported on 'Derby Tank Week' on 21 January 1918) to buy a tracked land tank or 'tank' – one of the new mechanised marvels. Sadly, though, its manufacture came too late to help in the war. Along with many others up and down the country, it was delivered to the town in triumph after the war, according to the *Derby Daily Telegraph*, and, after making it safe and removing the engine, it lived on Normanton Recreation Ground for many years before it was deemed an unsuitable war memorial. It was scrapped early in the Second World War and the metal was reused.

A postcard photograph of 6th Battalion Sherwood Foresters at Wool in Dorset, 1914, digging. The message on reverse reads: 'Dear A, sorry I did not come up on Christmas as B.S. came up on the same day I had to come back with kind regards wishing you all a bright and prosperous new year Private G E H x'. (© 2013 Derby Museums collection 1978-279)

Peace and Anti-War Protests

The most significant case of the anti-war movement in Derby is the trial and imprisonment of Independent Labour Party and Women's Social and Political Union (WSPU) member and anti-war campaigner, Alice Wheeldon of Pear Tree Road, Derby. A known

In June 1916, 748,587 men appealed to the Military Service Tribunal to avoid conscription. In October 1916, 1.12 million men nationally held tribunal (usually temporary) exemption or had cases pending and 1.8 million men had obtained war-work exemptions.

pacifist and helper of those trying to avoid conscription, she was targeted by MI5 agents, who tricked her into revealing her sympathies by presenting her with fake deserters. On 30 January 1917, Alice, her daughters Hettie and Winnie, as well as Winnie's husband, Alfred Mason, were all charged with conspiracy to murder the Liberal prime minister David Lloyd George and Labour Party cabinet minister Arthur Henderson. Alice was sentenced to ten years and was sent to Aylesbury Prison, where she went on hunger strike. At the request of Lloyd George, Alice was released from prison on licence on 31 December 1917. Her health permanently weakened, she died of influenza in 1919. Her case was reported heavily in the *Derby Daily Telegraph* throughout February and March 1917, often under the heading of 'The Great Conspiracy Charge', and was described as 'sensational' when news broke in January. In early 2013, a Blue Plaque was erected as a memorial at her home on 29 Pear Tree Road. The case has attracted much attention and it is thought by many that the Secret Intelligence Service fabricated much of the evidence.

3

WORK OF WAR

The Changing Face of Local Industry

Derby has long been an industrial and manufacturing centre, and it is perhaps one of the few left in the country still producing 'heavy industry' products and large-scale complex engineering items for export around the world today. Just before the First World War, however, it was not alone in this and counted Birmingham, Liverpool, Nottingham and Manchester among its rivals, specialising in iron and steel foundry, casting and other metal production, train manufacturing and textiles, alongside coal and other mineral mining in the wider county. All of these large industries were supported by a wealth of smaller engineering firms and manufactories (such as paint and varnish), as well as commercial businesses and produce trades (cheese, jam and milk) and the usual shops, markets and a fair number of estate agents and auctioneers.

The largest and most famous firms were Rolls-Royce, still going strong today – though no longer making motor cars in Derby – and the Midland Railway Locomotive Works and the Wagon & Carriage Works, whose legacy has been largely inherited by modern-day Bombardier. No less important in their day were Leys Malleable Castings Co. Ltd (the founder, Sir Francis Ley, famous for attempting to introduce American baseball to the UK, died during the war in 1916), Crown Derby (smaller than it had been in the eighteenth century, but still an important porcelain manufacturer and trading today as Royal Crown Derby) and the Derbyshire Building Society (now a part of Nationwide Building Society).

Looking at the trade directories of the period, particularly *Kelly's Directory of Derbyshire 1912*, you can get an immediate sense of which Derby businesses were thriving and growing just before the war and which had changed or indeed gone

Pages from the 1912 Kelly's Directory, showing some common types of Derby small business: iron foundry, tailoring and estate agents. (© 2013 Derby Museums)

Pages from the 1912 Kelly's Directory, showing adverts for Derby businesses, including Raleigh bikes. (© 2013 Derby Museums)

by the 1920s. These trade directories, especially *Kelly's*, were a cross between a Yellow Pages directory and a residential telephone book, and included advertisements not unlike modern equivalents. Unlike similar modern trade directories (superseded now to a large extent by the Internet, of course), the books also contained histories of areas, buildings, churches and civic organisations, making them an important snapshot of Derby. Some of the names are still familiar to us today, having only ceased trading recently, while others are long gone. Most of the street names and addresses are still there, albeit with different business now occupying the spot. The following is a list of some of the more important businesses before the war and after, with the descriptions lifted from *Kelly's Directory*:

Printers and Publishers
Bemrose & Sons Ltd – 'general and art printers, publishers and bookbinders, engravers and draughtsmen'. Main works: Midland Place, Derby, but also offices in Leeds, Manchester and London.

Bacon & Hudson Ltd – 'printers, stationers and book binders', Colyear Street. Appearing in the 1925 *Kelly's Directory* as a rival to Bemrose.

Shops, Tailors and Commercial Traders
Bennett Brothers (Derby) Ltd – 'wholesale and retail grocers', 99 St Peters Street (now a pharmacy), with a cheese factory on Bloom Street (now under the Intu shopping centre) and a provision unit at the Market Hall. Gone by 1925.

George Bennett – trading since 1734 in 'furnishings, general ironmongery, and kitchen ranges, stoves, chimneys, cutlery and sewing machines', 8 Iron Gate, Derby. Still there today and, judging by a recent visit, still trading in more or less the same goods.

Bracegirdle – 'furrier, costumier, mantle maker and milliner; ladies' knitted wear', 108–109 Friargate. Appearing after the war in the 1925 directory, indicating a rise in the demand for the 'luxury' end of fashion, in what their own advert states as 'high-grade goods', though 'all moderately priced'. Also one of the growing number of businesses in the directory to clearly state their telephone number: Derby 631.

In fact, the 1925 directory covers a number of larger adverts from tailors and men's and ladies' fashion providers, including Sol Lux, gentleman's tailor of St Peter's Street ('above Stead & Simpson in Nag's Head Yard') and James Potter & Sons of 61 Wardwick, formerly of The Strand, neither of which were in

Photograph of Irongate, Derby, around 1910, looking up towards All Saint's church. Bennetts would be on the right, behind the horse and cart. (© 2013 Derby Museums collection 1984-295)

View from The Spot down St Peter's Street, with Babington Lane coming in from the left. Derby Corporation electric tram No. 35 is ascending the hill. (© 2013 Derby Museums collection 1985-37/2)

Derby before the war. Others, like Kenneth Gregory – 'high-class Ladies' outfitter' trading as 'W. Gregory, Est. 1835', of 10 and 12 St James's Street – had been around before the war, but much more modestly described then as simply 'draper' and only at 10 St James's Street.

Brigden and Co. – civil, military and ladies' tailors, 27 Iron Gate. Now a public house. Trading before and after the war.

Derby Co-operative Provident Society Ltd (Co-op) – numerous branches all over the town and outlying areas. The Co-op closed its main department store on Exchange Street in 2013 after trading there for seventy years.

Pountain & Co. Ltd – wine and spirit merchants, Market Place buildings, Market Place and Wood Street.

Steel, Foundry, Iron Works and Heavy Manufacturing
Browns Foundry Co. Ltd – iron founders and stove and range manufacturers, Nelson Ironworks on Stockbrook Street and shop on 240 Abbey Street. Had a telephone in 1912 and one of the largest adverts in the 1912 *Kelly's Directory*.

Cox Brothers and Co. – lead merchants, Derby Lead Works.

Ley's Malleable Castings Co. Ltd – iron castings and foundry, Vulcan iron works, Osmaston Road.

Kitchen & Co. (Derby Boiler Co. Ltd) – boiler and heating apparatus makers, Mansfield Road. 'Repair riveted work with Speed, Merit, Economy.'

A newspaper advert for the Midland Drapery Co., St Peter's Street, from the Derby Daily Telegraph *on 11 November 1918. Note the comment about 'War Saving Certificates' at the bottom. (© 2014 Derby Evening Telegraph)*

W. Meakin & Son – railway milk churn and refrigerator makers, street lamps and stove pipe makers, Victoria Street.

Parker Foundry Co. Ltd – steel and malleable iron steel works. Brunswick works, Siddals Road, and Tropenas Works, Midland Road.

Banks and Financial
Berlitz School of Languages – Cumberland Chambers, 25 Wardwick, moving to 117 Friargate after the war. Still in business today.

London City & Midland Bank Ltd – several branches throughout the town, including St Peters Street. Later became Midland Bank PLC, and was later taken over by HSBC Holdings PLC, which still has a branch in St Peters Street.

J. Nutt & Sons – incorporated accountant, 12 The Strand. Just one of many firms and businesses dealing with financial matters. The 1911 census records 465 men as 'merchants, agents and accountants' in Derby, with a further 998 as 'commercial and business clerks' and 421 recorded as 'dealers in money and insurance', with women in these 'trades' making up an additional 465. What we would call the 'financial services industry' in Derby was as healthy as the textiles and metal manufacturing businesses.

Alliance Assurance Co. Ltd – Imperial chambers, Albert Street. Appears after the war.

Motor Cars and Cycles
Alvaston Motor Co. – motor car engineers, 1044 London Road.

Raleigh Cycle Co. – 80 St Peters Street (now a rather large bookshop). Raleigh is still going and has its headquarters in Nottingham, but no longer with a high-street shop in Derby.

Holmes & Co. – 'motor car body builders to His Majesty King George V', London Road. Elsewhere in the directory, the firm is described as having 'large workshops and extensive showrooms' covering 3.5 acres of ground.

View of Andrew Handyside and Co., Rolls-Royce's then-new works on Nightingale Road, Derby, 1907–1908. (© 2004 Derby Museums collection DMAG002064)

Mount Carmel Garage Ltd – 'motor garage engineers and electrical equipment specialists, repairs etc.', Burton Road.

Rolls-Royce – see main profile on p.60. Has a very modest entry in the 1912 directory, simply 'motor car manufacturers', Nightingale Road.

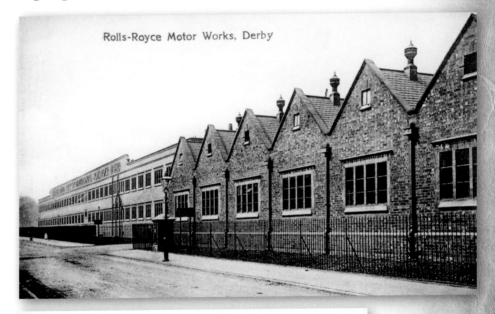

Rolls-Royce Motor Works, Derby

Rolls-Royce Motor Works, Nightingale Road, Derby, c. 1912. (© 2004 Derby Museums collection DMAG000978)

The interior of the Midland Railway Wagon and Carriage Works, around 1920. (© 2004 Derby Museums collection DMAG001963)

Artists and Makers

Lomas, Robert Gilbert (late Hall & Co.) – sculptor, marble mason and maker of fonts, 41 King Street, Derby. Appear in the 1912 directory and were still trading in 1925 with a large advert in the *Kelly's Directory* for that year, but now including 'memorials to special designs' and 'English alabaster bowls as applied to electric lighting', indicating that the firm had embraced the changing modern world.

Robert Tomlinson – cabinet maker and upholsterer, bedsteads and bedding, 44 Sadler Gate.

Midland Railway Locomotive Works and the Derby Carriage & Wagon Works.

***

Apart from Rolls-Royce, no other company did more for the war effort than the twinned companies of the Midland Railway Locomotive Works (focused around the station itself, including the roundhouse), making locomotive engines, and the Derby

Carriage & Wagon Works (further south, off Litchurch Lane) manufacturing 'rolling-stock', such as wagons and carriages. Both companies had started in the 1840s as the Midland Railway and split into the two parts in 1873.

By 1900, the Midland Railway Locomotive Works employed tens of thousands of people and produced some forty engines a year including, in 1907, the Paget Locomotive, an experimental steam locomotive using new techniques pioneered at the plant and designed by Sir Cecil Walter Paget, the General Superintendent and Chief Operating Officer of the Midland Railway. By 1910, electric power and lighting had been installed, which was provided by the company's own generating plant by Derby Canal. The company's premises were impressive and extensive, with numerous facilities, and a textile research facility was even opened in Calvert Street for upholstery and seat materials.

Sir Cecil Walter Paget (1874–1936), born at Sutton Bonington, was appointed General Superintendent of the Midland Railway in 1907. He served in France with the Railway Operating Division during the war, commanding operations in France and Belgium and rising to the rank of Lieutenant Colonel in the Royal Engineers.

In 1906, Paget designed and built an experimental steam locomotive with eight single-acting cylinders and rotary valves at Derby, which he financed himself but was completed by the Midland Railway. However, there was inadequate testing and remedial design work, and development stopped in 1909 and the remains were scrapped in 1915.

A photograph of 'Munitions Workers, Derby', taken by W.W. Winters during the latter part of the First World War. The company is unknown but the initials 'CB' appear in a plaque behind the predominantly female workforce. (© 2013 Derby Museums collection 1999–182/2)

Female munitions workers at the Midland Railway Locomotive Works working on the renovation of 18-pounder cartridge cases. The caption reads: 'Final inspection and packing.' (© 2013 Derby Museums collection L1991-440/1)

During the First World War, the works quickly turned to aiding the war effort, producing eleven howitzers by the end of the year. Derby produced a large number of shells (and reconditioned fired shells) and their components. Initially producing 3,000 fuses a week, production increased tenfold following the installation of automated equipment. A lot of the work was undertaken by women, as can be seen by a set of photographs taken at the site, showing women using machines and hand tools with minimum safety equipment and servicing and repairing fired 18-pounder shells ready for refilling with propellant. The factory is believed to have employed some 500 women.

Renovation of 18Pdr Cartridge Cases.
Final examination and packing.

Renovation of 18 P.dr Cartridge Cases.
Gauging.

1652

Just before the war, the Derby Carriage & Wagon Works produced 10- and 12-ton wagons in quantity. At the beginning of the day, a set of components would be made, and each would be assembled for painting by the end of the day. By 1919 – and using American mass-production methods – the company was producing 200 wagons and ten coaches a week. The sawmill at the site was recognised as the most modern and largest in Europe, with over 2,000 miles of timber being seasoned of nearly sixty different varieties.

In 1914, the works turned to producing supplies for the army, building ambulance trains and army wagons, as well as parts for rifles.

Female munitions workers at the Midland Railway Locomotive Works working on the renovation of 18-pounder cartridge cases. This caption reads: 'Gauging'. (© 2013 Derby Museums collection L1991-440/1)

59

Charles Rolls
and Rolls-Royce

Rolls-Royce was formed on 15 March 1906, by Charles Stewart Rolls (1877–1910) and Sir Frederick Henry Royce (1863–1933). Royce had been designing and making his own engines and cars in Manchester for some years and Rolls, a motoring and aviation pioneer, had his own car dealership. Together they would make world-famous luxury cars. Their actual partnership was short-lived, as in 1910 Rolls was the first Briton to be killed in a flying accident. By the time of their partnership, it was apparent that new premises were required for production of cars. It was an offer by the town council of cheap electricity that resulted in the decision to acquire a site on the southern edge of Derby.

The new factory was opened early in 1908, carrying on production of the famous 'Silver Ghost' model. The outbreak of the war caused the board to fear closure, as many of their orders came from Europe – orders that were unlikely to be paid for. Nevertheless, believing that war was likely to be short-lived, the directors initially decided not to seek government work making aero engines, something the now deceased Charles Rolls had tried unsuccessfully to persuade the company to do. The joint realities of their poor financial position and the fact the war was not going to be over quickly changed their minds and the company started to make engines under licence from Renault. Meanwhile, the Royal Aircraft Factory asked Rolls-Royce to design a new engine. Despite initial reluctance they agreed, and during 1915 developed the company's first aero engine – the twelve-cylinder Eagle. This was followed by the smaller Hawk, the Falcon and, just before the end of the war, the larger Condor.

Rolls-Royce expanded the Derby factory to cope with demand to build aero engines, and by the end of the war around half the aircraft engines used by the Allies were made by Rolls-Royce. By the late 1920s, aero engines made up most of Rolls-Royce's business.

The interior of the machine shop at Rolls-Royce Motor Works on Nightingale Road in Osmaston, c. 1912. (© 2004 Derby Museums collection DMAG000979)

British Celanese

One firm that came to Derby specifically due to the war was British Cellulose & Chemical Manufacturing Co., registered in 1916, to produce cellulose acetate. It was formed by Dr C. Dreyfus, a Swiss national, who had been invited to England by the British Government to make acetate 'dope', or lacquer, to his special patent, which was used to coat the fabric covering wings and fuselage of aeroplanes. Its principal manufacturing facility was at Spondon in Derby, which was built by Sir Robert McAlpine, with money from the War Office. It was a huge site – at least 121 hectares. By the end of the war, the company was known as British Celanese and at its height it employed many thousands of workers, producing acetate fibres after the war to make artificial fabrics that imitated silk. It closed for good on 14 November 2012. The site may be redeveloped (after decontamination) for homes and businesses.

Production output of the Midland Railway during the war:
9 ambulance trains completed
890 special wagons built
36 6" howitzer carriages built
11 8" howitzer carriages built
91 8" howitzer limbers complete
1,750 Army Service vehicles built
70 6-wheeled goods locomotives
6,128 railway wagons built
1,300,000 copper bands for 9.2", 8", 6" and 4.5" shells
2,600,000 shell fuses completed
6,500,000 18-pounder cartridge cases re-formed
400,000 steel stampings
180,000 guns and gun carriage components
273,500 components parts for Army Service vehicles

The Changing Role of Women (and Men) at Work

Some men were considered too valuable in their occupation to risk being killed during fighting. Indeed, some young men were barred from joining up on the basis that their 'war-work' was more important. In Derby, many employees of Roll-Royce, such as J.A. Moon of St Thomas' Road, were exempt from fighting. However, armbands and badges were necessary to ensure that individuals were not harassed in the street for being a 'coward' and certificates had to be carried to present to police and military authorities to ensure the men not in uniform were not spies or worse. These

men were the exception rather than the rule, though, and many soon found themselves outnumbered by women, who were sometimes in jobs they had never worked before.

The First World War is widely regarded to have advanced the rights of women economically and politically, but did the lives of ordinary women really change due to the war? As we have seen in Chapter 1, employment for women over the age of 10 years in Derby stood at about 31 per cent in the 1911 census, shockingly low by today's standards. Though classed as 'unoccupied', the 70-odd per cent who were not in work were housewives, looking after the children and running the household – a full-time job, without the benefit of modern labour-saving devices. There is no doubt that the war created short-term changes; between 1914 and 1918, an estimated 2 million women replaced men in employment, resulting in an increase in

A group believed to be Derby Gas Works workers, some just signed up and in uniform; others with 'war service exempt' badges. The back of the photograph says: 'Deadman's Lane: Gas Works: WW1 group.' (© 2013 Derby Museums collection 2013-112)

A war exemption armband, badge and certificates relating to J.A. Moon, a draftsman at Rolls-Royce. (© 2013 Derby Museums collections, 1982–373)

the proportion of women in total employment from 24 per cent nationally in July 1914 to 37 per cent by November 1918.

Some women had already been working in factories in Derby before the war and this can be seen clearly in the 1911 census. However, these were mainly in the textile industries and potteries rather than heavy engineering works, and they were normally younger, unmarried women. This changed with the war, with (initially) older women going back to the jobs they held before getting married, and later moving into areas that women had never worked in before, such as munitions (as we have seen at the Midland Railway), as well as more obvious wartime roles, such as nursing (see below), and roles previously reserved for men, such as bus and tram conductors and drivers. One such conductor was Mrs H. Davis of Allenton, who in late 1915 became the first of six Derby girls to serve on Derby's older open-top trams and occasional horse-drawn ones, too. According to her remembrances (recanted in local history newsletter *The Derby Ram*), she worked fifty-two hours a week in 1915, commencing her shift at 4.45 a.m. and receiving pay of 19s a week and often working in bad weather on the exposed, open top deck. She was even working the night of the Zeppelin attack in 1916 (*see* Chapter 5), getting stuck in freezing fog in the black-out before later hearing three men had been killed.

Hospitals and Charitable Institutions

Just before the war, Derby had a number of hospitals; some were very small, such as the Derbyshire Hospital for Women in Friargate (founded 1891, and in Bridge Street until 1907), with only twenty-five beds. Others were larger, like the Derbyshire Hospital for Sick Children (founded 1877) in North Street, with forty beds. There was also a Borough Infectious Hospital about 1.5 miles outside the town on Mansfield Road, with a sanatorium and a total of 162 beds, as well as a number of small charitable endeavours, such as the Licensed Victuallers' Asylum in Nottingham Road and Large's Hospital Charity in Friargate, providing specialist help.

Although not hospitals in the modern sense, organisations such as the Railway Servants' Orphanage on Ashbourne Road (which could hold 272 children), the Queen Victoria Memorial Home of Rest for incurable cases ('chiefly of consumption (TB), cancer and paralysis') and a convalescent home with twenty-eight beds at Holbrook (which later became a maternity hospital) did offer similar help. There was also the Derby Borough Asylum on Uttoxeter Road.

The main hospital, however, was the Derbyshire Royal Infirmary (now the site of the London Road Community Hospital), rebuilt in 1891 and opened by Queen Victoria, treating thousands of inpatients a year in many departments and 124,803 outpatient attendances in 1923.

War casualties (and medically sick) soon overwhelmed the existing medical facilities in England designed for civilian use. The field hospitals established in France – and so many civilian hospitals, asylums and convalescent homes, as well as many large buildings and former schools and stately homes – were turned over to military use to form war hospitals, including one in Derby (No. 4 The Military Hospital, Derby Barracks). Some military hospitals designed for that purpose already existed, such as the Queen Alexandra's Military Hospital, Millbank, which opened in 1907, or the Cambridge Military Hospital, Aldershot, which opened in 1879 and was the first base hospital to receive casualties directly from the Western Front, but there were none in Derbyshire. Some hospitals had been identified before the war for use by the Territorial Force as TF General Hospitals and were mobilised in August 1914. These were generally based at existing hospitals. For example, the 5th Northern General, a TF General Hospital in Leicester based at the old Leicestershire Lunatic Asylum, had room for 111 officers and 2,487 other ranks (the first Northern General was at Newcastle, the second at Leeds, the third at Sheffield and the fourth at Lincoln). All were expanded during wartime, and were often added to with auxiliary hospitals and annexes. They were staffed by a mixture of TF Nursing Service personnel and volunteers from many different organisations, such as the British Red Cross Society or the St John's Ambulance.

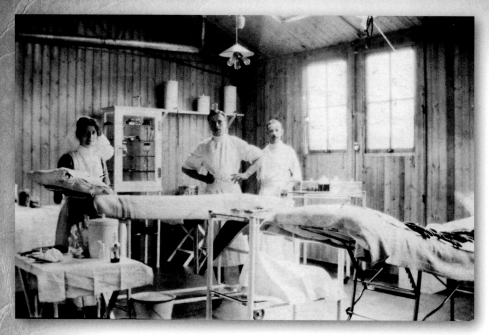

Operating theatre No. 10, General Hospital BEF Rouen, France, in 1915, with three medical staff, including one nurse showing operating tables and equipment. (© 2013 Derby Museums collection 1975-120/2)

The hospital system was divided into 'commands', and by 1917 the Northern Command, which included Leeds, Sheffield, Derby, Leicester, Lincoln and Nottingham, had an extensive auxiliary and Voluntary Aid Detachment (VAD) hospital system, with many small hospitals across the city and the county. This list is not exhaustive and is gleaned from many sources: Blackwell Auxiliary Hospital, Alfreton; Ashbourne VAD Hospital; Bakewell Red Cross Hospital; Belper VAD Hospital; Burton VAD Hospital and Burton General Infirmary; Devonshire Hospital and VAD Hospital, Buxton and Canadian Special Orthopedic Hospital (1917–19), Buxton; Aston Hall Hospital (near Aston-On-Trent, just outside Derby and probably the same site of a later 1930s psychiatric hospital that closed in the 1990s); Derby Royal Infirmary; Haye Leigh VAD Hospital, Derby (affiliated to 5th Northern General Hospital (T.F.), Leicester); Temple House VAD Hospital (formally at The Pavilion, Derby, and numbered Military Hospital 44, it may be the same as a small, modern NHS facility in Mill Hill Lane, Derby); Derbyshire convalescent home, Matlock; and Willersley Castle Hospital, Matlock.

Nursing in the First World War

There were a number of nursing organisations that took on the heavy burden of nursing the sick and wounded of the First World War. Some were voluntary and some were 'official'; some were linked to the military directly and some were 'civilian' in nature.

Queen Alexandra's Imperial Military Nursing Service (QAIMNS)
In March 1902, QAIMNS replaced, by royal warrant, the previous Army Nursing Service. This was not a huge organisation; in fact, there were only about 300 trained nurses at the outbreak of war in military hospitals around the world. Members of QAIMNS were all over the age of 25, single (or maybe widowed), educated, of good social standing and had completed a three-year course of nursing training in a hospital approved by the War Office. Although nearly 11,000 new nurses were recruited throughout the war, nearly all were as 'reservists', and therefore the 'permanent' establishment of 300 was never altered. These women also received training and were of a similar social standing. The women were often engaged on yearly contracts and most had been demobilised by the end of 1919, to return to civilian life.

The Territorial Force Nursing Service (TFNS)
The TFNS was formed in 1908 as a result of the Territorial and Reserve Forces Act of 1907. It provided nursing services for the home and reservist Territorial Force, and was intended to staff the territorial military hospitals in the UK. The women who enrolled in the service from 1909 were civilian nurses who continued to work in their 'peace-time' employment, but had agreed to be mobilised at short notice in case of war. Like the QAIMNS, the service expanded rapidly due to the war, with thousands of new nurses, and had similar standards of entry and training – even the uniform was similar. After the war, many TFNS nurses retained their status as a 'Territorial' and many were to return to nursing for the Second World War.

A postcard showing convalescent hospital inmates in 'blues' uniform, including one Sherwood Forester (with arm in sling, on right), 1914–18. The special uniform was designed to ensure that convalescing soldiers had a uniform they could wear in public to avoid any difficulty and harassment. (© 2013 Derby Museums collection 1990-43/3)

Queen Alexandra's Royal Naval Nursing Service (QARNS)

The smallest of the military nursing organisations, QARNS served military naval hospitals in Plymouth and Chatham. Just a few hundred nurses served in the First World War, but it expanded hugely during the Second World War.

Voluntary Aid Detachments (VAD)

In 1909, as a further measure to support the Territorial system, the War Office issued its 'Scheme for the Organisation of Voluntary Aid in England and Wales,' which set up both male and female VADs to fill gaps in the Territorial medical services. Many applied for this, but those created were often half-hearted organisations which never expected to be called upon for real. At the outbreak of war, the VAD detachments sprang into action in village halls, schools and other meeting places throughout the country. They were formed in small groups of just over twenty personnel and had to include at least two trained nurses. The untrained volunteers undertook the other duties necessary to run a small hospital: cleaning, cooking, setting up equipment and other small tasks. For many young, unmarried women, who may never have been alone and unchaperoned with a member of the opposite sex before, and who had to undress, wash and tend to young men, this was a daunting task.

During wartime, the VAD organisation was administered by the Joint War Committee of the British Red Cross Society and the Order of St John. It was run from Devonshire House in Piccadilly, loaned for the war by the Duke and Duchess of Devonshire.

It was not just wounds that soldiers had to contend with, but sickness and disease too, as this comment from Derbyshire Yeomanry Trooper Cooling illustrates:

Jan.5. [1916] Had to fall sick. Sent to Field Hospital then by Ambulance to Mina House Hospital. Feeling very bad. Scarcely able to speak. Complaint. Tonsillitis put to bed. Jan.7. One of the Tonsils breaks, but the other causes more swelling & pain. No sleep. Jan. 8. Miserable day on the whole. Although there is every attention paid to you. Very large aeroplane over Pyramid. Jan.9. Had to have it lanced. Terrible mess but the effects is grand. Can swallow with ease. Received 2 letters from Mary. Jan.10. Feeling grand after a good night's sleep. Put on Ordinary Diet.

Prisoners of War Camps and Prisons

Shortly after the outbreak of war, the War Office selected a number of places where prisoners would be held in internment. For the local area, a number of small camps appeared over the length of the war, including ones at Kegworth, Duffield (reported in the *Derby Daily Telegraph* on 10 July 1918 as a new camp); Ilkeston (Oakwell Colliery Buildings – a satellite of Burton-upon-Trent, opened on 1 July 1918 with thrity-one POWs), Sudbury, Shardlow (The Union Workhouse), Bretby (Bretby Hall Stables), Burton-upon-Trent, Ashby-de-la-Zouch, Crich (working at the quarry), Loughborough and Normanton, attached to Uppingham. No one is certain where this last one was, but it might have been in Normanton Park, which was demolished in 1925.

A photograph of a group of German prisoners of war from 172 Company. Message on reverse reads: 'In remembrance of the Great World War, Heinrich Matthej.' (© 2013 Derby Museums collection 1975-120/5)

Donnington Hall at Castle Donnington was one of the first places to be chosen by the War Office as a place of internment and was bought in 1915 as a big camp for 300 officers, though by the end of the war it held 1,000 officers and 300 men. It was quickly altered to have barbed wire and electricity, and furniture was provided. The commandant was a Lieutenant Colonel Picot, who looked after Prussian lancers, German naval officers and

airmen captured in the South of England. There were rumours of feasts and cocktails, polo matches and endless snooker and card games along with other tales of luxury care, but these were almost certainly not true. There was an escape committee, however, and several attempts to escape were made. The only success was Oberleutnant Gunter Pluschow who, along with another prisoner, stole bicycles and rode them to Derby, where they caught a train to St Pancras, London. The other man was captured and served forty-eight days' special detention, but Pluschow made it to Germany, where he was hailed a hero. He later denied the luxury, snooker and card playing, but did say that the camp had a lot of space. Thirty-four Germans died in internment and were buried there; the rest were returned in 1919. The Derby photographer W.W. Winters is believed to have visited and taken pictures of the men there, but unfortunately none of these survive in the Derby Museum collections.

4

NEWS FROM
THE FRONT LINE

The Sherwood Foresters

Although men from Derby and Derbyshire served in many
regiments – from the Royal Field Artillery to the Seaforth
Highlanders, from the Royal Fusiliers to the Royal Horse Guard,
and from the Royal Army Medical Core to the Royal Navy –
the majority of the pre-war Territorial Force and volunteer
battalions stationed and based in Derbyshire were part of the
Sherwood Foresters (Notts. & Derby) Regiment. In peacetime,
this regiment recruited mainly from Derby and Derbyshire and
Nottingham and Nottinghamshire. The vast majority of the men
of the Regular Battalions of the Sherwood Foresters who went
to France with the BEF and the Regular Army would have been
local. With the outbreak of war, all regiments recruited locally
and heavily and the Sherwood Foresters were no exception. Later
in the war, after conscription, men were not necessarily posted
together or locally and could serve in any regiment. Well over
140,000 men overall served in the Sherwood Foresters during the
whole war, and while not all were from Derby and Derbyshire,
the majority were from the area. Then, as today, the Sherwood
Foresters were considered very much a local regiment, held in
high regard with pride.

On the outbreak of war, the Territorial Army battalions of
Nottinghamshire and Derbyshire were all mobilised and men
rushed to enlist early on in August 1914. Battalions were formed

A postcard photograph of C Company (battalion unknown), Sherwood Foresters, somewhere in France 1914. (© 2013 Derby Museums collection 1998-199/9)

in Derby, Nottingham, Newark and Chesterfield. In peacetime, an infantry regiment of this era might have one or two regular battalions (of around 900 men each) who did the fighting (usually not together in the same place), and one or two more administrative or volunteer battalions that served as recruitment, training and reservist battalions, usually in the 'home' county or counties, and several Territorial Force battalions as 'weekend' soldiers – the same as the Territorial Army today. During the war, many new and replacement battalions were formed, and at one stage there were thirty-three battalions serving with the Sherwood Foresters, of which seventeen served overseas.

The 2nd (Regular) Battalion, who were in Sheffield at the outbreak of the war, were moved on mobilisation to Cambridge and deployed to France (landing 11 September 1914) to fight in one of the early battles of the war – Aisne in September 1914 (the First Battle of the Aisne was an Allied offensive against the German First and Second Armies as they retreated after the First Battle of the Marne). The 1st (Regular) Battalion, who had been in India, crossed over in November 1914. Both found themselves engaged in trench warfare shortly afterwards, as the movement and fluidity of the early war ground to a halt. In fact, it is during the Battle of the Aisne that trench warfare is credited

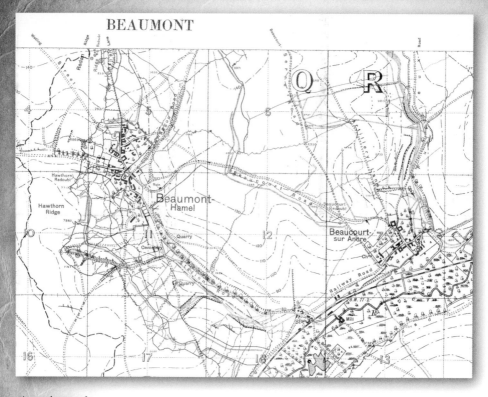

BEAUMONT

A trench map of the area around Beaumont, showing enemy positions and emplacements. (© 2013 Derby Museums collection L1973-231/4)

to have begun with Sir John French, who ordered the entire BEF to entrench. With that order, the tone and whole history of the war changed.

1915: The Battle of Loos

The end of 1914 saw trench lines – on both sides – running from the Swiss border to the English Channel, but they were not deemed permanent. The early battles of 1915 aimed to break through these trench lines, but were invariably unsuccessful. The Sherwood Foresters took part in one of these early battles in Neuve Chappelle (10–13 March 1915) in the Artois region of France. The British did break through but were unable to exploit the success. Despite this, the numbers of troops arriving from Britain enabled a continuous British line to be formed, from Givenchy-lès-la-Bassée north to Langemarck. On 10 March 1914, Sherwood Forster Private Jacob Rivers of Derby won the Victoria Cross. The Battle of Loos (25 September to 14 October 1915)

German barbed-wire entanglements – an invention perfected for the First World War. (© Sherwood Foresters Museum Collection, 2000-3570-36)

was the largest British offensive mounted on the Western Front in 1915. The battle was the first mass engagement of the largely all-volunteer New Army (or Kitchener's Army) units and marked the first British use of poison gas. The British offensive was part of a French attempt to break through the German defences in Artois and Champagne and force a war of movement. Despite better equipment and improved tactics, the Franco-British attacks were contained by the German armies. Casualties were high on both sides; an estimated 60,000 losses on the Allied side and 26,000 for the Germans.

As part of the 46th Division, the 139th Brigade – made up of battalions of the Sherwood Foresters – were involved in the battle for the strongly fortified position of the Hohenzollern Redoubt, a separate objective within the Battle of Loos. The British 9th Division captured the redoubt and then lost it to a German counter-attack. The fresh troops of the 46th Division were sent in on 13 October under the cover of gas, but the

The 46th North Midland (NM) Division was made up of the 137th (Staffordshire) Brigade, 138th (Lincoln & Leicester) Brigade and the 139th (Sherwood Forester) Brigade; the 1st, 2nd and 3rd NM Field Ambulance; 4th NM (Howitzer) Brigade, Royal Field Artillery (RFA); field companies of the Royal Engineers and other units.

assault failed and resulted in 3,643 casualties, mostly in the first few minutes. It was here that Captain Geoffrey Vickers of the Sherwood Foresters won the Victoria Cross for his actions on 14 October 1915. Ultimately, the combatants made no progress and the Battle of Loos was over.

Elsewhere, in Turkey, the 9th Battalion Sherwood Foresters took part in the ill-fated landings at Gallipoli between April 1915 and January 1916.

1916: The Battle of the Somme

The main battle in 1916 for the Sherwood Foresters was the Battle of the Somme, which started on 1 July. After a lengthy bombardment of the German lines, 'a walk over' was promised but by the time the battle ended, the British Army had suffered over 600,000 casualties, of which 108,700 had been killed. The battle was one of the largest of the war, in which more than 1 million men were wounded or killed on all sides in total, making it one of humanity's bloodiest battles and one the most synonymous with the perceived pointlessness of the First World War in general.

The initiative on the Western Front was taken by the Germans, who launched a massive attack against the French at Verdun in February. In order to support the French and relieve pressure on their army, the British attacked at the Somme on 1 July. Despite a previous heavy artillery bombardment on the German trenches, 20,000 British soldiers died while fighting the Battle of Albert in what is called 'the first day on the Somme'. The entire 46th (North Midland) Division, which included the 139th Brigade (Nottinghamshire & Derbyshire), attacked Gommecourt on 1 July as a diversion, also suffering heavy casualties. The Sherwood Foresters almost missed this battle, however; on 27 December, the division was ordered to Egypt (likely to join troops in Gallipoli) and its units were despatched south to Marseilles. However, these orders were soon cancelled. On 20 April, the division was withdrawn from the line at Vimy and was ordered south to make ready for the attack on Gommecourt.

The division was in fact in a weakened state. Drafts to replace the casualties at the Hohenzollern Redoubt had been slow in arriving and many new officers had no experience of the Western Front. The division was also ravaged by serious illness: typhoid, paratyphoid, trench fever and diphtheria. Again the attack failed and the Germans were successful in holding their ground.

1917: Third Battle of Ypres, or Passchendaele

On 31 July the British launched an offensive in Belgium officially called the Third Battle of Ypres, but which became known as Passchendaele. The battle took place on the Western Front, between July and November 1917, for control of the ridges south and east of the Belgian city of Ypres in West Flanders. The imagery from this battle – shell-cratered ground which had been churned into a sea of mud, with trees stripped of their branches – has become, along with barbed wire and poison gas, one of the principle memorable images of the war. Here, the Germans used mustard gas for the first time in the war. The British Army, meanwhile, lost over 60,000 men.

The 139th (Sherwood Forester) Brigade was made up of the 1/5th, 1/6th, 2/7th and 2/8th Battalions, Sherwood Foresters and from 1916 was joined by 139th Machine Gun Company and 139th Trench Mortar Battery. It was briefly joined in 1915 by the 1/4th Battalion, the Black Watch and the 1/3rd Battalion, the London Regiment.

A photograph of Sanctuary Wood near Ypres, taken between August and October 1917, shows tree stumps, trenches, holes and some men near a sandbag bunker. (© Sherwood Foresters Museum Collection, 2000-3570-25)

1918

The Russian Revolution of 1917 ultimately led to the end of the war with Russia on the Eastern Front and enabled the German Army to achieve a transfer of troops and firepower to the Western Front. On 21 March 1918, the Germans launched an attack which penetrated the British line to a depth of 40 miles within a week. Sherwood Forester battalions were involved in the heavy fighting which finally succeeded in halting the German advance. The Foresters played a prominent role in the subsequent Allied counteroffensive, which led to the breaking of the German lines.

The End of the War

1919 saw many battalions disbanded, as men who had enlisted 'for hostilities only' were returned home for demobilisation. This process continued into 1919 as the army readjusted to its peacetime structure. As would happen in later years, 'welcome home' parades were held in Nottingham and Derby, where cheering crowds greeted the returning soldiers. The 1st and 2nd Regular battalions had to be made up to strength and the

1st moved to Ireland. In the autumn of 1919, the 2nd Battalion began a tour of Foreign Service which was to last for seventeen years.

The Derbyshire Yeomanry

On 4 August 1914, all yeomen were ordered to 'mobilise', and the squadrons from Chesterfield and Bakewell reported to Derby within days to assemble. Most of the men were farmers, quarrymen and colliers, who brought their own pit ponies. The Yeomanry was formed into a 'War Establishment' of three squadrons of 147 officers and men, a machine-gun section, signallers and a transport section, and were assigned to the 2nd Mounted Division. Intensive training took place near Reading. Swords were issued and in November the regiment moved to the Norfolk coast because of the fear of invasion. They would remain there until 1915.

SHERWOOD FORESTERS' CASUALTIES.

The casualty lists published this (Monday) morning contain the names of the following Sherwood Foresters:—

OFFICERS WOUNDED.
Sec.-lieut. N. L. Hindley, 8th Sherwoods (T.F.).
Sec.-lieut. G. S. Rivington, 6th Sherwoods (T.F.).

KILLED.
Private W. Skipper (13442), 1st Sherwoods.
Private W. Walters (20009), 1st Sherwoods.

DIED OF WOUNDS.
Private F. Costall (4774), 1st Sherwoods.
Corpl. H. A. Cottee (10875), 1st Sherwoods.
Private H. Groome (13882), 1st Sherwoods.
Private J. Hilton (11062), 1st Sherwoods.
Private A. E. Atterbury (708), 6th Sherwoods.
Private C. Cooper (2595), 6th Sherwoods.

DIED OF GAS POISONING.
Driver J. W. Stevens (286), 1st N.M.F.C. (T.F.).

WOUNDED.
L-cpl. R. A. Blower (11762), 1st Sherwoods.
Private P. Corcoran (10413), 1st Sherwoods.
Private W. Jones (7612), 1st Sherwoods.
Private J. Richmond (7782), 1st Sherwoods.
Private S. Currey (6257), 2nd Sherwoods.
L-cpl. H. Hutchinson (4519), 2nd Sherwoods.
Private J. Keenan (4937), 2nd Sherwoods.
Cpl. E. E. Peet (5855), 2nd Sherwoods.
Private W. Smith (3571), 2nd Sherwoods.
Private J. Brown (10182), 1st Sherwoods.

BOWLS.

Markeaton v. Mafeking Hotel.— An interesting game was played on Saturday afternoon and evening between the players of the Mafeking Hotel Bowling Green and the Markeaton Recreation Bowls Club, resulting in a win for the Mafeking. A very pleasant time was spent in a spirit of friendly rivalry, and the thoughtfulness of the proprietor of the hotel (Mr. Parkinson) in providing light refreshments for the players was much appreciated. A return match is to be played at Markeaton in a fortnight's time. Score:—

Markeaton.		Mafeking.	
Laverock, Guest, and Cowley	9	Parkinson, Reps, and Lilley	31
Smith, Delves, and Gadsby	26	Perkin, Canham, and Mayhieu	31
Garratt, Eccleshaw, and Redfern	11	Hall, Nixon, and Penn	31
A. Garratt, Nix, and Lowe	25	Hy. Gerrard, H. Gerrard, Ward	31
	71		124

A reportage of Sherwood Foresters casualties in the Derby Daily Telegraph *in August 1915. Note the rather surreal placement next to the bowls results. (© 2014 Derby Evening Telegraph)*

Derbyshire Yeomanry on horseback, just before the war. (© 2013 Derby Museums collection 1990-87/1)

Derbyshire Yeomanry soldiers in a courtyard in Cromer. The text written on reverse reads: 'Derbyshire Yeomanry, Imperial Hotel, Cromer, Jan 29th 1915, My dear Bro and Sis I arrived back safely and I'm just about settled down again. I hope you are well as there is quite a bit of illness about just now and also amongst us. I feel sure you will be able to pick me out on the other side without marking it I was just going to put a feed on my horse you will see the nose bag at my feet … With my best love to you all your loving Bro John.' (© 2013 Derby Museums collection 2003-188/4)

The 2nd Mounted Division was made up of the 1st South Midland Mounted Brigade, 2nd South Midland Mounted Brigade, London Mounted Brigade and the Nottinghamshire and Derbyshire Mounted Brigade, along with 2nd Mounted Division Train, medical, signal, veterinary and RFA components.

Gallipoli

In August 1915, Winston Churchill (then Secretary of State for War) ordered the attack on the Dardanelles to open a sea route to Russia. The Yeomanry were first sent to Egypt in 1915, but were immediately ordered to Gallipoli (without horses) and landed on the Turkish Gallipoli Peninsula at Sulva Bay. Their division was ordered to attack Chocolate Hill and the Yeomanry advanced under a Turkish barrage. With heavy casualties and all attacks having failed, the campaign quickly developed into trench warfare. They had to endure high temperatures, poor food, snipers, rationed water and swarms of flies. The regiment returned to Egypt on 28 November, leaving the Australian and New Zealand Corps (ANZAC) to carry on until December 1915.

Derbyshire Yeomanry in Egypt. (© 2013 NCOs Derby Museums collection un-accessioned image)

1916: Salonika

An expeditionary force, including a mounted Derbyshire Yeomanry, was landed in Northern Greece at Salonika to fight the Bulgarian army and draw off German troops from the Western Front. Salonika is mountainous and could therefore be easily defended. The Allied force consisted of units of the British, French and Greek armies totalling 100,000 men against a combined force of Germans, Turks, and Bulgarians of nearly 500,000 strong. After many defeats, the Allies advanced slowly toward the Bulgarian frontier. Conditions were dreadful, with snow and mud and men sleeping in the open with little forage for the horses.

The following lines are taken from Trooper Cooling's diary:

Feb.7 [1916]. Landed, proceed from Salonika at 9am. Mounted arrive at Akbuner Camp about 6 miles from the City. Prep. Horse lines at camp. Warned for Main Guard at night.

Feb.8. Main Guard all day good nights rest bitter cold.

Feb.10. Camp routine as usual, very cold night. Sent letters.

Feb.11. Line Guard all day, very cold . Patrol for the Squadron.

Feb.12. Exercise for the horses very cold & bad day, raining. Night horse line guard, bitter cold weather. First issue of rum.

Feb.13. Sunday. Exercise, tobacco served out, also water-proof cloke [*sic*] & cap cover, fur gloves. Dry day.

Derbyshire Yeomanry Trooper Cooling's diary.
(© 2013 Derby Museums collection 2013-126)

A page from a photograph album showing the Derbyshire Yeomanry in Salonkia engaged in the tricky business of moving horses around.
(© 2013 Derby Museums collection 2004-827/49)

For the next two years, the Derbyshire Yeomanry fought in Salonika against the Bulgarian and Turkish forces, but remained on horseback. They carried out many mounted patrols in villages and on bridges in the Struma Valley. Unlike at Gallipoli, traditional cavalry actions were possible, but these were small scale compared with the wars of the Victorian period. It was a dangerous time, with constant risk of ambushes from Bulgarians disguised as Greek villagers; from the Greeks themselves, whose loyalties were mixed; and from wolves. The Yeomanry were often under attack from German aircraft and had to improvise anti-aircraft methods.

Horse Shunting. English Quay.
SALONIKA. 1918.

We return to Trooper Cooling's diary:

> July.16. [1916]. We go out on patrol. I am one of the 4 picked to go as advanced guard at 3.30am. We start & skirmish our way up to Bikova & make the village secure for the troops to enter. Our troop remains in the village in support. Men under Lt William go to the village of Butkova-Juma to ascertain if the village is held by Bulgars. They get within 30 yards of the village when they are fired on. The horses all bolt and 5 of the men are dismounted but the enemy do not follow up the attack. One man is shot through the shoulder, but not very serious. All the horses are caught & the men get into safety without any further mishap. Nothing to report for rest of the day.

1918: *The Beginning of the End*

In July 1918, the Allies took the offensive. For the first time the attack succeeded and Turkish forces retreated. The Derbyshire Yeomanry followed the retreating enemy into the foothills of Salonika through mountains and ravines until they entered Bulgaria. In September, peace envoys bearing white flags were seen and peace was declared on 1 October. Although the war, for the Yeomanry, was over, the winter of 1918–19 was unpleasant, with influenza taking many lives. By April 1919 they had been demobilised and by May 1919 they were all back home to a civic welcome in Derby. The future of the Yeomanry was uncertain, but in 1922, the regiment became an armoured car regiment.

Nottinghamshire and Derbyshire Mounted Brigade (later numbered as the 7th Mounted Brigade) was made up of the Sherwood Rangers Yeomanry, the South Nottinghamshire Hussars and the Derbyshire Yeomanry (the 1/1st, cavalry; the 2/1st – a home cyclist unit – from 1916, and the 3/1st – a home training unit).

Letters Home: News from the Front

Right from the start, thought was put into how soldiers would communicate with their loved ones back home, and there was an immediate concern about censorship and what soldiers might say about

NOTHING is to be written on this side except
the date and signature of the sender. Sentences
not required may be erased. If anything else is
added the post card will be destroyed.

[Postage must be prepaid on any letter or post card
addressed to the sender of this card.]

I am quite well.

I have been admitted into hospital

$\begin{Bmatrix} sick \\ wounded \end{Bmatrix}$ *and am going on well.*
and hope to be discharged soon.

I am being sent down to the base.

I have received your $\begin{Bmatrix} letter\ dated\_\_\_\_\ \_\_\_\_\_ \\ telegram\ ,,\ _____ \\ parcel\ \ ,,\ _____ \end{Bmatrix}$

Letter follows at first opportunity.

I have received no letter from you

$\begin{Bmatrix} lately. \\ for\ a\ long\ time. \end{Bmatrix}$

Signature $\begin{Bmatrix} \\ \end{Bmatrix}$
only

*Date*_____

(94890) Wt. W1566-R1619 14,000m. 6/17. J.J.K. & Co., Ltd.

A Field Service postcard – Army Form A2042. (© 2013 Derby Museums collection 1984-994/3)

the war. Perhaps initially, this was not so much that the authorities were concerned that the soldiers would tell their loved ones seditious or disloyal things, but rather information that could be used by enemy spies. Army Form A2042, otherwise known as the Field Service Post Card or FSPC, was the answer (discussed in the August edition of the *Derby Mercury*, where the system is explained under the heading: 'Army Secrecy – how British Soldiers' letters may be sent and received'). It carried on the address side an imprint of a penny stamp, and on the back a series of messages which could either be crossed through and 'deleted' or kept. Basic information could be conveyed to the recipient about the sender's well-being without the need for the card to be censored. The soldier was not allowed to write anything on it except his name and the date, and was warned that 'if anything else is added the postcard will be destroyed'. FSPC were printed on buff-coloured card, although some also appeared on blue, red and green.

When free postage was introduced, the one-penny FSPC was replaced by a card without the imprint. At first they were rationed to two a week, but this was later relaxed and the cards were issued on request. They were – perhaps unsurprisingly – popular during periods of heavy fighting. As they were not liable to much scrutiny, the cards travelled through the postal system more swiftly than any other types of mail and were known as 'wizz-bangs'. In early 1917, members of the BEF sent nearly 130,000 a day and by autumn, the figure had risen to over 285,000. It is estimated that at its peak, the war postal service processed over 12 million letters a week.

To monitor morale and to ensure that ordinary handwritten mail sent by soldiers on active service contained no useful information should it fall into enemy hands, letters were subject to censorship, usually by one or more junior officers of the regiment or the battalion. After being handed in unsealed, the letter was read, passed, countersigned and then handed to the officer in charge of the unit censor stamp. There were several ways to censor a piece of correspondence: a blue pencil was frequently used to strike through an offending word or sentence – sometimes whole portions of a letter were cut – and often the name of a town or village depicted on a picture postcard was scrubbed out with a sharp instrument.

Very quickly, soldiers began to send ordinary letters and postcards, but these were definitely censored and soldiers had to take care in what they said; many ended up saying not much at all, other than basic pleasantries and sentiments of care and love, which perhaps was all that was needed. The example below is from a postcard postmarked 22 May 1916, from Private Albert Dyke to his mother in Derby. It says:

> Somewhere in France. Dear Mother, just a line to let you know I am alright and in the pink at present. I hope you are going on alright. It has been grand weather here this last week so finish with best love from your loving son Bert. xxxxxxxxxxxxxxxx

Another, undated, says:

> To Daddy's little girlie with Dad's best love and kisses. Take care of my little laddie and help your Mum all you can and Dad will not forget his bonnie darlings. Ta ta for now. Best love from Dad. Xxxxxxxxxxxxxx

Sadly Albert was killed on 6 June 1916, while serving with the Sherwood Foresters on the Somme.

Later on, special 'On Active Service' envelopes were provided, on which the writer had to sign on their 'honour' that the contents were nothing but personal and relating to family matters only.

The following is an extract from a letter dated 28 October 1918 letter from Fred Woodward to his wife in Abbey Street, Derby (though it is clear he has just seen her on leave). It sums up a lot of the war and the feelings it generated:

My Dear Gert ... just saying that I am back with the Batt and jolly glad too ... I don't feel half so rotten now I'm with the boys again. I hope you are quite well kid and not feeling the recoil too much. I know while I was at the base and at Dover, I felt simply awful. Things don't look so hopeful as regards peace now or is it with me being over here, for the war is still on, just as usual ... I expect you are thinking of going home again ... let me know if there is any news about the allowance won't you? I'm looking out for another letter from you ... So long dearest. All my love, Fred.

And, continuing before the above was sent:

This is Sunday, and I'm in hospital ... for I got in the way of a few spare bits of iron yesterday morning ... I was operated on yesterday and had them removed. I am feeling pretty fit now dear so don't worry and besides I think it will be a Blightly [return home] almost sure. I'm being treated fine here; they're all so kind, well so long for the present.

An example of an embroidered postcard. This one is addressed: 'To my dear mother.' The message on the reverse reads: 'With love, Will. BEF March 26th 1917.' (© 2013 Derby Museums collection 1978-14/1.8)

A postcard from Private A.H. Dyke to his mother in Derby. You can clearly see the censor mark and, reading the text, he is not really saying anything at all. (© 2013 Derby Museums collection 1985-257/1.2)

An Active Service envelope for sending personal mail. This one was sent to Mrs Woodward by her husband Fred, who was seriously wounded in 1918. (© 2013 Derby Museums collection 1978-14/2a)

Fred wasn't sent home, but his optimism that he was 'fine' was to be short-lived for, on 6 November 1918, a telegram was sent informing his family that he was dangerously ill at hospital from gunshot wounds, though he ultimately pulled through and survived the war.

LIFE IN THE TRENCHES

A soldier of the Derbyshire Yeomanry wrote on 15 September 1915 that 'digging formed the chief part of our existence, with colliers in the Regiment we dug splendidly'.

From 1915, trench life dominated the life of the infantryman and the dismounted cavalryman. The trenches formed a network of defences, varying from deep bunkers to shell holes, linked by shallow diggings. As the war went on, these became deeper and more sophisticated and formed a series of lines stretching back to the safer rear zones. Rebuilding was constant, as enemy artillery and mortars destroyed many trenches and the links between them.

It is one of the myths of the First World War that soldiers spent months or years in the front line in constant combat. In fact, battalions were rotated between front-line duty and the rear, spending many days at each, probably only spending three days a month right at the front and ten days a month in the trench system. This might increase during a battle or a counter-attack, but even then the men were often relieved by new troops. It was not uncommon to spend a month or more in the rear in relative safety.

Trenches were also often flooded and were overrun with rats. Sanitation and decent cooking facilities were non-existent; the men were dirty and infested with lice. Futhermore, the threat from shelling and enemy sniping was constant. Noise, fear and tension were always present and sleep scarce. In the east, at Gallipoli (Turkey) and Salonika (Greece), soldiers also had to contend with flies and extreme heat.

Combat in the trenches – if the enemy reached that far – was fierce and frantic, and possibly accompanied by gas and initial mortar and shellfire. With long-barrelled rifles a liability in close quarters, the men had to use bayonets, 'trench-clubs' and heavy calibre pistols to fight hand-to-hand.

Unknown officer eating in an Allied trench.
© 2008 Derby Museums collection IMGP0615.

Wipers Times

The *Wipers Times* was a trench magazine produced by British soldiers from the 12th Battalion Sherwood Foresters, initially while based on the front line at Ypres, Belgium. The soldiers came across an abandoned printing press and a sergeant who had been a printer in peacetime salvaged it and printed a sample page. The paper itself was named after how the soldiers thought you should pronounce 'Ypres' ('why-pers', rather than 'eep').

A lot of the men involved are unrecorded, but the main editors are known to be Captain (later Lieutenant Colonel) F. J. Roberts and Lieutenant F. H. Pearson. Most other contributors used pseudonyms, which had double meanings satirising contemporary newspaper pundits. The *Wipers Times* also frequently made use of ironic initials such as P.B.I. (Poor Bloody Infantry).

The paper consisted of poems, jokes and cartoons, witty and wry reflections, and lampoons of the military situation on the Western Front. It maintained a humorously ironic and slightly subversive style that today can be recognised in satirical magazines such as *Private Eye*.

War Poetry

Today, one of the most recognisable products of the First World War is poetry.

Perhaps for the first time in a conflict, a substantial number of important, already-published English poets were volunteer and conscripted soldiers at the same time, writing about their experiences of war. Many of these died on the battlefield, most famously Wilfred Owen. Others, including Robert Graves and Siegfried Sassoon, survived but were scarred by their experiences, and this was reflected in their poetry and other writings.

Many works by British war poets were published in newspapers and anthologies, and proved very popular, though the tone of the poetry changed as the war progressed. In many respects, the poetry represented a 'safe' way of bringing the horrors of war to the attention of the public and providing a hidden critique of those who had put them in that situation. Other poems are purely patriotic, with no hidden agendas.

One of these poets with local connections is T.P. Cameron Wilson (1888–1918), who wrote the famous 'Magpies in Picardy', published 16 August 1916. Cameron Wilson was commissioned into the Sherwood Foresters and reached the Western Front in February 1916. He was killed at Hermies in France and has no known grave. He is commemorated on the lychgate at St Paul's church, Little Eaton, Derbyshire, just outside Derby. A writer and poet before war broke out, he was particularly affected by what he saw. Cameron Wilson wrote poetry throughout the war, finally losing his life in 1918. He will always be remembered for 'Magpies in Picardy', the first verse of which is below:

> The magpies in Picardy
> Are more than I can tell.
> They flicker down the dusty roads
> And cast a magic spell
> On the men who march through Picardy,
> Through Picardy to hell.

Conscientious Objectors

The concept of a Conscientious Objector (or CO) is a complex one and is often defined as an 'individual who has claimed the right to refuse to perform military service' on the grounds of a moral, conscious and/or religious standpoint. In peacetime during the early twentieth century, this was not an issue because the UK did not have a National Service. However, in wartime, with conscription being introduced (the Military Service Act of March 1916), COs were suddenly a problem.

The Military Service Act specifically allowed for COs to be absolutely exempted, to perform alternative civilian service, or to serve as a non-combatant in the army, but they first had to convince a Military Service Tribunal that their reasons were genuine.

Around 16,000 men were recorded as official COs, with traditionally pacifist persons such as Quakers being the majority. What is perhaps surprising is the number of cases heard in front of the tribunal, which is believed to be around 750,000 – not all of these were COs or even claiming to be; the tribunals were there to hear claims regarding medical and employment exceptions as well. Despite the Act appearing to take into account the moral choices of individuals, the tribunals were notoriously harsh towards those claiming to be COs, reflecting widespread public opinion that they were lazy, or cowards seeking to benefit from the sacrifices of others. Therefore the vast majority of cases were rejected. Of the 16,000 recorded COs, many of these were sent to do 'work of national importance', such as farming, or were ordered to undertake non-combat duties (the ones the tribunals considered genuine). However, around 6,000 were forced into the army, and when or if they refused orders, they were sent to prison.

Many objectors accepted non-combatant service, for example working as stretcher bearers. COs who were deemed not to have made any useful contribution lost the vote for five years after the war, but this was hard to enforce.

One local example is Arthur Herbert Ludlow, who was born in Derby but lived in Crich Common and worked as a clerk for the Midland Railway in Derby. He was a lifelong Quaker and a member of the Sherwood Foresters, though he refused to serve. He was called up on 19 May 1917, aged 35, although he declined a medical examination and was not granted CO status. He was tried twice in 1917 for disobeying orders and imprisoned both times. Finally, Ludlow was discharged for being no longer physically fit for war service, but this was due to his disability rather than his beliefs.

Sedition and Mutiny

Outright sedition and mutiny by British forces is rare, but one of the most infamous mutineers of the First World War was Percy Toplis, who allegedly took part in the Étaples Mutiny of 1917 in France. Originally from South Normanton, near Chesterfield,

Derbyshire, he was known as the 'The Monocled Mutineer' on account of him impersonating officers in order to gain access to their pay, using a gold monocle as part of his disguise. He even gave press interviews in the UK about his war experiences when 'on leave', infamously in Blackwell, which appeared in the *Nottingham Evening Post*. Originally a stretcher bearer in the Royal Army Medical Corp, he deserted and, it is believed, regularly moved between regiments masquerading as an NCO or an officer in order to get food and money. He is supposed to have been a leading participant in the mutiny (which took place at the training camp known as The Bull Ring at Étaples). Although Toplis was sought in France following the mutiny and posters for his arrest were issued, his actual involvement is debated by historians. He was shot and killed in Cumberland in 1920 after again impersonating an officer and allegedly killing a taxi driver.

5

HOME FIRES BURNING

Rationing and Food Shortages

Unlike rationing in the Second World War, which was long-term and affected almost all products and goods from the beginning, rationing in the First World War was a very different affair and was not introduced fully until the beginning of 1918. At the outbreak of the war, people 'panic bought' and began hoarding, so much so that very early on some shops run out of food. However, after the initial shock of war, people fell into a routine ('Food Panic Ending', *Derby Daily Telegraph*, 7 August 1914) and shortages appear to have been rare in the first few years of the war, although price increases were common.

The Defence of the Realm Act (*see* Chapter 2), among many other things, was designed to gently deal with and prevent shortages, without actually imposing rationing. A voluntary scheme where people limited their own intake, led by example by the Royal Family was also tried, but it was not entirely successful. By 1916, the situation had deteriorated and Britain had only a few weeks left of wheat and grain for bread; for the first time, shortages seemed very real and prices rose sharply. The people of Derby did not take all this laying down, though; there was the occasional protest and complaint about food price increases, such as the Railway Women's Guild's march through the town, protesting against the high prices of food (*Derby Daily Telegraph*, 15 December 1915).

Britain continued to import food from overseas – Canada and the USA in particular – and, for a while, these voyages were relatively safe. However, in 1917, Germany introduced unrestricted submarine (U-boat) warfare and suddenly, with losses (including the RMS *Lusitania*, which was sunk in 1915 with the loss of over 1,000 lives, some of whom are commemorated at St Matthew's church, Darley Abbey) rising in the Atlantic Ocean, things looked very bad. As in the Second World War, any area that could grow food was converted to do so; gardens were turned into allotments and chickens were kept in back gardens. Using powers under DORA, the government took over millions of acres of land for farming. With the men away, the work was often undertaken by the Women's Land Army (WLA). Conscientious objectors were also forced to work on the land.

Despite all this, the impact of the German U-boat campaign made food shortages a serious problem by 1918. Malnutrition was seen in poor communities and, as a result, the government introduced rationing in 1918; food products were added to the list as the year progressed. In January 1918, sugar was rationed and by the end of April meat, butter, cheese and margarine were included. Ration cards were issued and everyone had to register with a butcher and grocer. This tactic worked; the malnutrition that had been identified earlier disappeared and no one actually starved in Britain during the war. Occasionally, food shortages caused other problems, such as the Baker's Strike in Derby in August 1919, where the bakers of the Co-operative society complained

Ministry of Food ration books issued to J.R., J.A. and T. Moon of 230 St Thomas' Road, Derby, in October 1918. Many of the stamps have been used but those that are left are for lard and jam. (© 2013 Derby Museums collections, 1982-373)

about shortages. The accompanying editorial reads: 'meanwhile queues are to be seen at the various shops as there is a shortage of bread at many stores' (*Derby Daily Telegraph*, 7 August 1919). Rationing ended in 1920.

Zeppelin Raid

On the night of 31 January 1916 a new form of warfare came to Derby, forever shattering the notion that civilians were safe far behind the front lines at 'home' and ushering in a new term: 'strategic bombing', a tactic that would cause so many civilian deaths during the Second World War. The Germans had a not-so-secret weapon: Zeppelins – mighty cigar-shaped airships with a rigid body and filled with flammable hydrogen gas to create lift. These ships, designed and built by Count von Zeppelin, were used for commercial and passenger flight before the war and were considered the height of sophisticated travel. That changed in January 1915, when a German Navy airship launched the first-ever strategic bombing raid on civilian targets in the UK (Great Yarmouth and King's Lynn), changing warfare forever.

At the end of January 1916, a force of nine (although reported at the time as six or seven) airships, commanded by Korvettenkapitan (Captain) Peter Strasser, chief of the Marine Luftschiff Abteilung (German Naval Airship Division), set out to attack Liverpool. On that foggy night, bombs fell across the Midlands as the airships hit Walsall, Dudley, Tipton, Wednesbury, Derby and Burton-on-Trent (but none of their actual targets) on either solo missions or working in tandem. The official figures released at the time puts the total casualties of this raid at fifty-nine deaths (thirty-three men, twenty women and six children) and 101 injured, though early newspaper reports played this down by instead emphasising that 'no considerable damage has been reported' (*Derby Daily Telegraph*, repeating a War Office statement of 1 February 1916 under the headline 'Last Night's Raid'). Some later reports put the casualties at

Zeppelin banner L21 that took part in the East Midlands raid on the night of 31 January 1916. (© 2013 Derby Museums collection 2010-95/3)

sixty-one dead and 101 injured across the whole East Midlands. This was not the first Zeppelin raid reported by the *Derby Daily Telegraph* that week; only the previous day the paper had reported on a raid on Paris where, although 'no serious damage was done', twenty-five people were killed.

That night in 1915 saw the first and, thankfully, last Zepplin raid where death and destruction had occurred in Derby itself.

The very first account in the same edition of the paper reveals more:

The War Office issue the following; the air raid of last night was attempted upon an extensive scale, but it appears that the raiders were hampered by a thick mist. After crossing the coast the Zeppelins appeared at various quarters and dropped bombs at several towns and in rural districts in Derbyshire, Leicestershire, and Staffordshire. Some damage to property was caused, but no accurate reports were received until a very late hour.

The first detailed report of the damage of the Midlands raid came from an official War Office statement printed in the *Derby Daily Telegraph* on 3 February 1916:

One church and a congregational Chapel were badly damaged and a parish room wrecked. Fourteen houses were demolished and a great number damaged, less seri-ously by the doors, window panes, etc., being blown out. Some damage, not very serious, was caused to railway property into places. Only two factories, neither being of military importance, and a brewery, were badly damaged and two or three other factories were slightly damaged. Bombs dropped: the total number of bombs discovered up to the present exceeds 300. Many of them fell in rural places where no damage was caused at all.

Not surprisingly, the rest of the week in the local newspapers was dominated by the raid, including advice about protection, such as 'The Zeppelin Peril – lower your lights – warning to the public', advising that shopkeepers and others reduce lights at night. There was also a spirited complaint from a member of the public writing to the *Derby Daily Telegraph* on 1 February 1916, stating that although some works' lights in the Rosehill district were put out due to the warning of airships, the Reginald Street Baths were left brilliantly illuminated and asked the important question: 'Does the local lighting order apply only to tradesmen and private residents while exempting the property of the Municipal Council?' The council, seemingly, did not reply.

We know from subsequent accounts that at 7.30 p.m. on the night of 31 January a buzzer was sounded. Some steps were taken to reduce light but, as the airships failed to appear straight away, it was possible people thought it was a false alarm and some may have been turned back on. Two days later, adverts began to appear in the *Derby Daily Telegraph* for 'Zeppelin Insurance' offered via the *Daily Mail* under the banner 'Protect yourself today', supplying the reassurance of money awarded if you were killed in a raid.

Around this time, the *Derby Daily Telegraph* also began to comment on German announcements, under the heading 'Strange German Claims'. It seemed that German newspapers had declared that bombs had been dropped in Liverpool, Manchester, Nottingham and Sheffield – causing 'mighty' explosions and a lot of damage, in addition claiming that all the Zeppelins made it home. On 3 February 1916, the *Derby Daily Telegraph* also provided an unverified translation of a German account, which could easily have been made-up propaganda designed to stir up an angry populace:

> … then the Zeppelins came out of the night and taught this naughty people that war can overtake them everywhere, and that it is bloody, terrible and serious. England's industry to a considerable extent lies in ruins. England's own soil has been ploughed by the mighty explosive shells of the German Air Squadrons. Over England there was a fierce and hard fought battle … and it was won by German Airships. They returned proud and sound. England can now contemplate their ruined centres of her industry and trade to which he has been brought by this wicked policy of her statesmen.

On 5 February 1916, the *Derby Daily Telegraph* printed a detailed but simultaneously vague account of the damage caused in the raid and lists, without qualifying exactly where the damage

Remains of Zeppelin bombs were to be found for many years afterwards, as this disturbing photograph of two children shows. (© 2013 Derby Museums collection 2010-95/5)

was caused, each piece (for example 'one Engine shed' and a 'railway grain shed') ending with the lofty and superior statement: 'It is not proposed in the future to issue detailed statements of this character, as it is inadvisable to give information to the enemy.' Zeppelins did not return to Derby.

It was not until the end of the war that the *Derby Daily Telegraph* returned to the raid and provided, for the first time, accurate and detailed accounts of exactly what happened. The events of that night have been researched many times and, over the decades, the *Derby Daily Telegraph* and others have published many eyewitness accounts and other details that help us get a picture of what happened that night. We know that it was Zeppelin L14 that attacked Derby and that four men were killed, three outright on the spot from one bomb and another man from his wounds three days later. A woman also died from a heart attack that night, but it is unclear if this was due to terror of the Zeppelins or just coincidence.

Zeppelin Banner L14 statistics: Class-P Zeppelin. A crew of 18. Length 163.5m, diameter 18.7m. Power 4x Maybach CX engines. Max. speed 97.2 km/h (60.4 mph). Range 4,300km (2,670 miles). Service ceiling 2,800m (9186ft). Flew 42 reconnaissance missions. 17 attacks on Britain. Dropped 22,045kg of bombs. Destroyed by crew 23 June 1919. Most successful German Navy airship of war.

Of the total of nine Zeppelins that took part in the raid, we know the movements of some of them. It is known that L21 was spotted close to Derby at 6.45 p.m., but didn't attack; L13 likewise at about 7.45 p.m. and L20 at about 8.35 p.m. Shortly after, Burton was attacked, likely by L20 and – it is believed – also by L19 and L13 between 8.45 p.m. and 9.45 p.m. L20 also bombed Stanton Ironworks near Ilkeston at around 8.20 p.m. It was L14, commanded by Kapitänleutnant Alois Böcker, that returned a few minutes after midnight to attack Derby.

It is estimated that around twenty-one high-explosive bombs and four incendiary bombs were dropped on Derby. Compiling all the available information, it seems that the main target was the area south of the train station: Osmaston Road and areas around the Roll-Royce works. To give a more detailed picture, high-explosive bombs fell on Midland Railway Locomotive Works, near No. 9 Shed (killing three men outright and one from wounds later); units belonging to the Wagon & Carriage

A destroyed Zeppelin. Those Zeppelins not shot down or destroyed by Britain and her Allies were destroyed by their own crews in 1919. (© 2013 Derby Museums collection 2010-95/4)

Department; Derby Lamp Company in Gresham Street, damaging finishing goods; the Rolls-Royce track near the workshops; and some on adjacent land. Incendiary bombs fell on the yard of Fletcher's lace factory in Osmaston Road, another near Bateman Street, and several more in Horton Street, setting one house alight. A mix of high-explosive and incendiary bombs fell on a coal heap at the Derby Gas Company's Litchurch premises but failed to ignite it.

There was an inquest immediately afterwards and quite a lot of attention was placed on the lighting of the areas and who controlled it, with suggestions that the police take responsibility for it from now on. The jury found that 'the deceased were killed by a bomb from a German Zeppelin'; their final comments (as reported in the *Derbyshire Advertiser*, 11 February 1916) were as follows:

The jury express their sympathy with the relatives and friends of the four victims of one of the most murderous outrages the country has ever witnessed and we hope that, when the day comes, England and her Allies will not forget the outrageous crimes that have been dealt out to their civil population.

The men who died in the Zeppelin raid were William Bancroft (32), a fitter of 34 Strutt Street; Harry Hithersay (23) of 73 Devonshire Street; James Gibbs Hardy (56), an engine driver of 11 Strutt Street; and Charles Henry Champion (48), a fitter, from 33 Fleet Street, who died three days later from his wounds.

When the raids began, the British defences were totally inadequate to deal with the Zeppelin threat. However, by 1916, a range of anti-airship defence measures had been introduced: guns were deployed, as well as searchlights and radio interception techniques. Finally, fighter aircraft were also sent against them and it was soon realised that Zeppelins were extremely vulnerable to explosive shells, which set light to the hydrogen, with spectacular results. Zeppelin raids were called off in 1917, by which time seventy-seven out of the 115 German Zeppelins had been shot down or totally disabled. By the end of the war, over 1,500 British citizens had been killed in air raids.

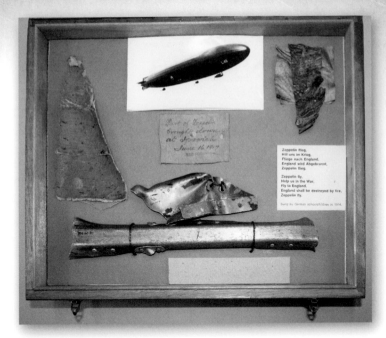

The remains of a Zeppelin (L48) brought down on 16 June 1917, 'near Ipswich', but actually near Holly Tree Farm in Therberton, near Leiston, Suffolk. (© 2013 Derby Museums collection 1980-722/60)

Spy Hunting

There were always rumours that German spies were abroad in the UK, gathering intelligence on the British war effort and guiding Zeppelins in the attacks on British towns and cities, and the Derby raid was no exception. One man who took steps to hunt down spies in his own time was W. Harold Hoare, councilman and later mayor of Derby. While on holiday in 1915, he observed the suspicious behaviour of a young man writing letters very slowly in a 'West Country' holiday resort. Following the man for many days, Hoare managed to acquire the blotter from which a letter was written, and thus the intended address. It was only then that he contacted the police and a watch was placed on the man and the address in east Suffolk. Arrests followed; it transpired that all who were involved were part of a German spy cell signalling to Zeppelins. Hoare received a letter of thanks and appreciation of his services from the police authorities, but the story did not become public until the 1930s.

VICTORIA CROSS WINNERS

Four Victoria Crosses were awarded during the First World War to soldiers with strong local connections.

The first was Corporal Fred Greaves VC, 9th Battalion Sherwood Foresters. Born in Killamarsh, Derbyshire, he died in Brimington in 1973 and is commemorated at the crematorium there. The medal is held at the Sherwood Forester Museum, Nottingham. On 4 October 1917 at Poelcapelle, near Ypres, Greaves attacked a machine gun in a stronghold with bombs; later the same day, with all the officers dead or wounded, he took command of the company and set up defences against a counter-attack.

Bombardier Charles Edwin Stone VC, 83rd Brigade Royal Field Artillery, was born in Ripley, Derbyshire, and died in Derby in 1952. He is buried at Belper Cemetery and his medal is at the Royal Artillery Museum, Woolwich. On 21 March 1918 at Caprine Farm, France, after working his gun for six hours, Stone was sent back to the rear with orders – returning with a rifle to hold up the enemy under machine-gun fire to protect his own guns. Later, he captured a machine gun and four prisoners.

Sergeant William Gregg VC, 13th Battalion of the Rifle Brigade, born in Heanor, Derbyshire, and dying there in 1969, is commemorated at Heanor Crematorium. His medal is at the Green Jackets Museums in Winchester. Gregg also won the Distinguished Conduct Medal and Military Medal and served in the Second World War as a Sergeant Major. On 6 May 1918 at Bucquoy, France, he rushed two enemy machine-gun posts, knocking them out and capturing the guns and gun teams. Later, he led an attack against another machine gun and later still led another successful charge against the enemy.

Private Jacob Rivers VC, 1st Battalion, Sherwood Foresters, born in Wideyard Gate, Derby, in 1881 is commemorated on the Le Touvet Memorial Panel 26–27 and has no grave, as his remains were not found. He was killed in action on 12 March 1915, aged 33, at Neuve Chapelle, France. On that day he attacked a large group of the enemy with bombs as they prepared to attack the flank of his battalion, causing them to withdraw. He repeated this later the same day, but was killed.

A Victoria Cross medal. (Library of Congress, LC-DIG-npcc-05387)

Football

Derby County FC were generally a Division One team and started there in the first divisional season in 1892/93, until being demoted at the end of the 1907/08 season to Division Two. They went back up for the 1912/13 season and stayed for the 1913/14 season (which ended on Saturday, 25 April 1914, where they drew 1–1 away at Newcastle United) but lost that position once again, finishing bottom, just as war broke out.

They played at Derby Baseball Ground (also known as Ley's Baseball Ground), close to present-day Osmaston Road and the bombardier works. It was built by Sir Francis Ley as a stadium for his factory workers from Ley's Malleable Castings Vulcan Ironworks. It was used as a baseball ground between 1890 and 1898 as Ley tried – rather unsuccessfully – to introduce American baseball to the UK and football from 1896 (which overlapped with baseball for a while) until 1997, when the old stadium was replaced with the current Pride Park Stadium. The old stadium was demolished in 2003/04 to make way for

Derby Baseball Ground. Alderman Laurie kicks off the ladies' charity football match, 1922. (© 2004 Derby Museums collection DMAG002069)

modern housing – the closest street today to the site, not surprisingly, is called Baseball Drive.

Despite the outbreak of war, Derby County FC played an ordinary 1914/15 Football League Division Two season, with ex-player Jimmy Methuen acting as manager from Wednesday 2 September 1914, on which day the team played at home against Barnsley, winning 7–0. They were back in Division Two, where they had arrived after demotion from Division One the previous season. Regardless of what was going on in Europe, they seemed to play every week without fail, winning most of their matches (Jimmy Moore was the top goal scorer of the season), particularly when they were at home, and finished first in the league, technically winning promotion. Unfortunately, this was to be the last 'normal' season for a while.

The football authorities attracted some criticism for deciding to carry on with the league, and were accused of being 'unpatriotic'. The league was suspended fully after this one full wartime championship, though Derby FC played a season in the wartime Midland's Section during 1915/16 before closing down for good. Some players continued playing for a while longer with Notts County, however.

Many of the players, both those who had played for the club in the past and those more recent, went on to serve and fight in the war. There are a couple of individuals, though, that have tragic and interesting tales and are worth mentioning in more detail. The first is Bernard Vann, a schoolteacher and chaplain who played as centre forward for the club in the 1906/07 season for a total of three games (having played previously for Northampton Town FC and Burton United FC). On the outbreak of war, he joined the 28th (County of London) Battalion, the Artists Rifles as a private and was soon commissioned as a second lieutenant in the 1/8th Battalion, the Sherwood Foresters. He was awarded the Military Cross twice, before winning the Victoria Cross posthumously for his actions on 29 September 1918 at Bellenglise and Lehaucourt, France, where he led his battalion across the Canal de Saint-Quentin. He was killed in action; shot by a sniper at Ramicourt, on 3 October 1918.

Derby Country FC is one of the founding twelve members of the Football League in 1888. It is one of only ten clubs to have played in every season of the English Football League. The team currently play in the Championship League, where they ranked 10th in the 2012/13 season.

The second footballer worth mentioning is legend Steve Bloomer. He had the singular misfortune of having just retired from Derby County FC at the end of the 1913/14 season, after a successful home and international career, to secure a job as coach and instructor of Berlin Britannia FC. He arrived there to take up his post with exceptional bad timing on 14 July 1914 and was immediately caught up in the war (his plight was documented back home in the *Derby Daily Telegraph*, 'Steve Bloomer still in Berlin', 7 August 1914). At first, British nationals abroad were treated with some respect, but eventually this changed and Bloomer was arrested on 5 November 1914 and sent to Ruhleben Civilian Internment Camp just outside Berlin. The camp detainees included 4,000 to 5,000 male citizens of the Allies who had been living, studying, working or on holiday in Germany at the outbreak of the war. They also included the crews of several civilian ships stranded in German harbours or captured at sea, and fishermen captured from trawlers who were mainly from Hull, Grimsby and Boston. The camp was basic and some of the living quarters were ex-stable blocks and haylofts, but – rather infuriatingly for the Germans – the prisoners with English 'stiff upper lip' and 'make do' attitudes made the best of it, and Bloomer spent most of his time playing football (leading his barrack's team to victory). He was released in March 1918, went back to Derby as a player and later coached in a number of capabilities for many years. He died in 1938. Bloomer remains a legend at Derby County and the club anthem, 'Steve Bloomer's Watchin'', is played before every home game. There is a bust of him at Pride Park Stadium, which was unveiled in January 2009.

The normal league recommenced on Saturday, 30 August 1919, with Derby FC playing at home against Manchester United, drawing 1–1. They stayed in Division One for the next year also, but were demoted for the 1921/22 season.

Cricket

It is the sport of English cricket that, for most people, conjures up an idyllic image of the myth of the Edwardian period – hot summers and well-spoken and classically educated gentlemen sportsmen playing non-competitively on the village green, with no poverty or trouble in sight. While that image is not quite true, the early twentieth century was certainly the 'golden age' of English cricket. Sadly, like so many things, this was about to end. The outbreak of war ended first-class cricket almost immediately and the County Championship was suspended until the 1919 season. A few clubs tried to hold matches and carry on at first, especially after the MCC (Marylebone Cricket Club, or Lord's, the cricket authority) issued a statement on 6 August 1914, stating that 'no good purpose can be saved at the moment by cancelling matches', but attendances started to drop and players were called away to join their regiments (many as officers) or chose to volunteer for the first time. Cricket was very popular indeed in the 1910s and, despite trouble brewing in Europe, over 14,000 people turned out to watch Jack Hobbs, one of the era's greatest batsmen, achieve a career best of 226 on 3 August 1914, a bank holiday and the day before Britain declared war on Germany. Things changed rapidly

Railway Servants Orphanage, Recreation Field, Ashbourne Road, 1913. This image shows the boys' cricket match in front of the pavilion. (© 2004 Derby Museums collection DMAG000057)

however, with the Oval soon being requisitioned by the military, the pavilion at Old Trafford transformed into a Red Cross hospital and then, on 13 August 1914, another statement from the MCC, saying that due to the war, all matches at Lord's would be cancelled (although a few county games carried on).

Within a few weeks, casualties from the front were mounting and concerns grew that it was wrong to carry on. The famous W.C. Grace wrote in *The Sportsman* on 27 August declaring that it was 'not fitting' that able-bodied men should play when they should be signing up. Public opinion moved against the notion of cricket continuing and so, finally, the MCC 'ended play'; the last match of first-class cricket was held on 2 September 1914, between Sussex and Yorkshire.

This is not to imply that all cricket stopped. Play continued as special matches, such as the Midlands match of the 1st North Midlands Field Ambulance RAMC officers *v.* sergeants, which occurred on 25 August 1914 at Harpenden, Derbyshire, or the Lord's matches in July 1917 of the English Army XI *v.* Australian Imperial Forces. Other attempts seem bizarre: for example, the author Robert Graves (*I, Claudius*) recounts falling bullets from machine-gun fire from aeroplanes rather inconveniently stopping play in France in 1915 at Vermelles, when a bird cage with a dead parrot inside was used as the wicket. This almost certainly did not happen, or it was exaggerated; it is likely that the author played on the ridiculous absurdity of the war as he saw it.

It is believed about 210 first-class cricketers, who were regular club players in the 1910s at the County Club and Test level, fought in the war, with thirty-four of them killed. Out of the 220-plus first-class and test cricketers who had ever played who were killed in the First World War, Derbyshire County Cricket Club were relatively lucky to have only five veterans of the club killed: all officers but one and only one regular player who was active just before the war. These were:

Captain Frank Bingham (1874–1914) from Alfreton, killed at Ypres in Belgium while serving with the 5th Battalion, King's Own Royal Regiment (Lancaster). He had played only once for the club in 1896.

The staff of Derby School: some in military uniform, others in academic dress. Geoffrey Jackson may be among them. (© 2013 Derby Museums collection 2010-53/1)

Lance Corporal Arthur Marsden (1880–1916) from Buxton, killed while serving with the 12th Battalion, Manchester Regiment. He appeared for Derbyshire in 1910.

Lieutenant Charles Newcombe (1891–1915) from Great Yarmouth, killed in action in France with the 7th Battalion, King's Own Yorkshire Light Infantry. He played only once for the club, but he was also a footballer who played for Chesterfield FC 1910–1912.

Captain Guy Wilson (1882–1917) from Melbourne, Derbyshire, killed while serving with the 1st Derbyshire Howitzer Battery RFA at the Battle of Cambrai. He went to Derby School between 1892 and 1901, where he also played cricket as captain of the school team. Wilson went on to play a couple of times for the Derbyshire Country Cricket Club in the early 1900s.

Geoffrey Jackson (1894–1917), born Birkenhead, Cheshire, died at the Battle of Arras after being wounded by shell fragments while serving with the Rifle Brigade. Jackson played for Derbyshire from 1912 to 1914, as well as for Oxford University in 1914.

Founded in 1870, Derbyshire Cricket Club's first president was the Earl of Chesterfield and G.H. Strutt acted as vice president. Today, it plays at County Cricket Ground, previously known as the Racecourse Ground. Derbyshire was once considered one of the weakest clubs in English cricket, having lost every single match between 1897 and 1920.

Geoffrey Jackson was related to two other players who fought in the First World War, but did not play cricket for the county until afterwards. Guy Jackson (1896–1966) served as lieutenant and later captain with the 1st Derbyshire Yeomanry and was awarded the Military Cross in 1918. He played for the county 1919–36.

Sir Anthony Mather-Jackson (1899–1983) served with the Grenadier Guards and first played for Derbyshire 1920–27. Sir Anthony is in turn related to Henry Mather-Jackson (1894–1928), who served with the 9th Lancers during the First World War and whose uniform is displayed at Derby Museum.

Amusements in Derby

Boys at Derby School in the early twentieth century, training as cadets with Lee Enfield .303 rifles. (© 2013 Derby Museums collection 2010-53/8)

Every edition of the *Derby Daily Telegraph* in the war years contained a section entitled 'Amusements in Derby', mainly focusing on the theatre and 'picture houses' or cinemas, all of which are now gone. Regularly, there were notices of a concert or band, such as the Band of HM Royal Marines, which played at Normanton Recreation Ground and Derby Arboretum

(*Derby Daily Telegraph*, 7 July 1916), or other events such as talks ('Mass Meeting of Railway Clerks at the co-operative Hall in Exchange Street' to 'discuss salary and bonus questions and after-the-war problems', *Derby Daily Telegraph*, 16 October 1917), and exhibitions and shows ('Derby Mothercraft Exhibition at the Temperance Hall', *Derby Daily Telegraph*, 16 October 1917) along with various annual shows. Largely, however, the notices relate to plays, music, musical comedies, dance and 'moving pictures'. Some of the movies appear familiar to us, such as the classic filmed-many-times action movie, *The Prisoner of Zenda*, which played at White Hall Cinema in August 1915. Others, such as Lieutenant Cherry Kearton's film *Across Central Africa* at the Victoria Electric Theatre, are similar to the kind of documentary more likely to be on television today, rather than at the cinema. Other 'picture houses' included the Cosy, the Alexandria, Babington Lane Picture House and the Normanton Picture Palace. The theatre had a similar range of presentations and productions; for example, Fred Kitchen and his company produced *All Eyes* at the Grand Theatre, Derby, in August 1915, while the Five Sisters act put on music and dance in between and 'burlesque character comedians' played at the Hippodrome. At the Pavilion in June 1916, there was the comedy play *The Glad Idlers,* which apparently was a 'show warranted to drive dull care away' (*Derby Daily Telegraph*, 10 June 1916). In 1917, the Hippodrome was still going strong, with the 'Femina Quartette' being advertised in October 1917 followed by the mysterious 'The Wonderful Zomah', while the Grant Theatre had a long-running farce called *A Little Bit of Fluff.* All this indicates that Derby and Derbians enjoyed a range of 'normal', non-war related activities and entertainments and were able to have fun despite the difficulties and horrors of the war.

6

COMING HOME

The beginning of the end: the Derby Daily Telegraph *headline on 6 November 1918. (© 2014 Derby Evening Telegraph)*

'The Great Carnival of Slaughter was over'

Cessation of hostilities took effect at 11 a.m. on the Western Front – the 'eleventh hour of the eleventh day of the eleventh month' of 1918. While this is often used as the official date to mark the end of the war, it actually reflects a ceasefire on the Western Front rather than an end to the war itself. Hostilities continued in other regions, especially across the former Russian Empire and in parts of the old Ottoman Empire. The war officially ended with the signing of the Treaty of Versailles on 28 June 1919.

In the run-up to the Armistice, the papers begin to indicate the end of the war, with headlines such as 'Germany and Peace – delegates leave Berlin to meet Foch' (*Derby Daily Telegraph*, 6 November 1918), as well as demonstrating that this was a British victory ('The Great British Victory – German Defences broken on thirty mile front. Enemy in full retreat'). The newspapers also gave their readers details of what would happen next, including war pensions ('what wives and dependents ought to know') and hints on the future of Votes for Women (*Derby Daily Telegraph*, 7 November 1918). As 11 November approached, more details appeared: 'The Armistice – terms being considered', with warnings about the British military situation, as well as talk of revolutionary action in Germany and mutiny amongst its military ('The Revolutionary Movement in Germany – Naval mutiny spreading', *Derby Daily Telegraph*, 8 November 1918), as well as accounts of fighting that was still going on.

Then, on 11 November: 'The End of the War – hostilities are to cease on all fronts at 11am today.' And with that, the war was over. Alongside this simple statement are other notices and headlines, revealing the immediate effect: 'Local Peace Rejoicings – remarkable street demonstrations', 'Flags and bunting and great crowds', 'Lighting Restrictions Relaxed' and 'Calling Up Notices Cancelled'. There was talk of industry and factories returning to civilian output – all on the same day. There was clearly celebration: 'Fireworks, Bonfires and Church Bells – the Chief Constable has received a telegram from the Commander-in-Chief Northern Command, that permission is granted for fireworks or bonfires, and Church bells to be rung at all times for a period of one week.'

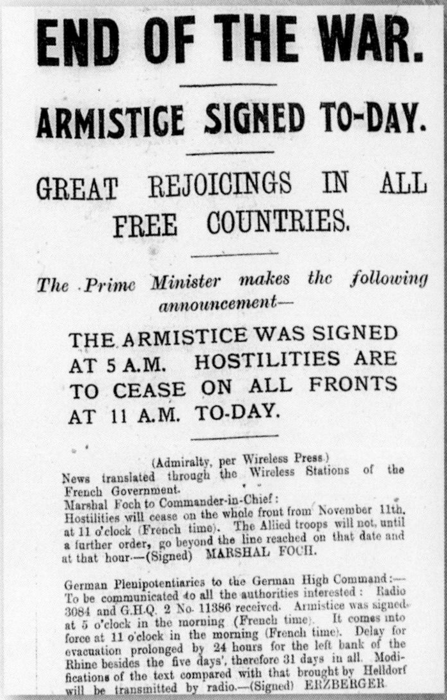

The *Derby Daily Telegraph* reacted soberly:

> The announcement that the armistice has been signed and that the great carnival of slaughter was over, was received everywhere with feelings of great thankfulness and joy. To us British, who have accomplished the grand purpose for which we took up arms there is special cause for rejoicing, and the scenes in Derby to-day may be taken as typical of what has happened in all parts of the Kingdom.

The celebrations started again in 1919 with the 'true' end of the war and the Treaty of Versailles, and the *Derby Daily Telegraph* was full of various articles and reportages throughout

The Armistice is announced, 11 November 1918. (© 2014 Derby Evening Telegraph)

The newspaper clipping reads:

END OF THE WAR.

ARMISTICE SIGNED TO-DAY.

GREAT REJOICINGS IN ALL FREE COUNTRIES.

The Prime Minister makes the following announcement—

THE ARMISTICE WAS SIGNED AT 5 A.M. HOSTILITIES ARE TO CEASE ON ALL FRONTS AT 11 A.M. TO-DAY.

(Admiralty, per Wireless Press.)
News translated through the Wireless Stations of the French Government.

Marshal Foch to Commander-in-Chief:
Hostilities will cease on the whole front from November 11th, at 11 o'clock (French time). The Allied troops will not, until a further order, go beyond the line reached on that date and at that hour.—(Signed) MARSHAL FOCH.

German Plenipotentiaries to the German High Command:—To be communicated to all the authorities interested : Radio 3084 and G.H.Q. 2 No. 11386 received. Armistice was signed at 5 o'clock in the morning (French time). It comes into force at 11 o'clock in the morning (French time). Delay for evacuation prolonged by 24 hours for the left bank of the Rhine besides the five days', therefore 31 days in all. Modifications of the text compared with that brought by Helldorf will be transmitted by radio.—(Signed) ERZBERGER.

A postcard of the Peace Carnival on 9 July 1919, held in Derby to celebrate the end of the First World War. Taken at Cheapside, just outside where the modern entrance to Derby Museum and Art Gallery would be. (© 2013 Derby Museum Collection, 2002-140/2)

July 1919 about what was termed the 'Peace Celebrations' and 'Victory Marches', which included religious services, marches of veterans ('March of Derby's Heroes'), bands and special events. These included a 'Public Thanksgiving Day and United Service of Thanksgiving for Peace', which was held at the arboretum on 6 July 1919 (*Derby Daily Telegraph*, 4 July 1919); a peace service at St Andrew's church; a peace celebration at Allestree; a 'Peace Sunday' service at All Saint's church, also on 6 July, which – similar to memorial and commemorative services today – was attended by many important guests and dignitaries and representatives of public bodies. The *Derby Daily Telegraph* of 8 July 1919 details some of the events (and on 17 July begins to set out what it called the 'Peace Time Table') which were going to occur on 18 and 19 July 1919, which appears to have been an all-day carnival with sporting events, a flower show, a regatta, bands, a swimming gala, processions of discharged men, soldiers' and sailors' entertainments, decorations and illuminations and, if that was not enough, a boxing match. Various organisations and firms made additional arrangements and even the Poor Law Guardians ensured the inmates of the workhouse were able to take part.

Readjustment and Re-Employment

There is no doubt that all soldiers of all sides must have been happy and relieved to be going home to wives, children and families, but there must have been a sense of apprehension too. Many of the returning soldiers, and those who had returned already, were recovering from horrendous wounds and it is estimated that at least 80,000 of them were disabled to a severe degree; many suffering from loss of limbs or sight and with disfiguring scars from gas attack. Others would have been suffering from initially invisible psychological disorders, referred to in this era as 'shell shock'. There was hunger due to food shortages (*see* Chapter 5) and the real threat of unemployment, despite some women returning to their old roles as housewives. There also must have been a sense of fear: will I be treated as a returning hero? Or just the opposite: will I be despised as a murderer and warmonger?

The help the men got depended on who they were. It appears that for officers, quite a lot of advice and support was given. The best evidence of this was the book *A Record of Opportunity as to Careers and Training*, published in November 1918 by 'The Appointments Department, The Ministry of Labour'. This was designed 'for the use of serving officers of HM forces … in regard to their resettlement in civil life when war service is ended or drawing to an end', and talks of training and the new 'opportunities' the men might have as the result of the war. It is a very optimistic booklet, considering the scale of death and destruction, but perhaps they had little choice but to look to the future with a positive view.

The foreword, written by the Minister of Labour, talks of the need to restore to full strength 'the educated man-power of the country as represented largely by the officers who will be returning to civil life, and by men of similar education who have chosen to serve their country in the ranks'. Do not forget, this was a different age where only those of certain 'middle-class' backgrounds went to university

Both sides used poison gas in the war. Chlorine gas, first used in 1915, killed outright. Phosgene gas killed days later with no immediate effect, and mustard gas (1917) blinded, burnt the skin and lungs but was not always fatal. The British experienced 188,000 gas casualties but only 8,100 fatalities.

and entered professions. This book was not to help the ordinary soldier, but those of the elite educated and 'gentlemen' classes, who had been the core of the officer class in the war.

The book makes plain that the nation had 'lost a very heavy proportion of the men who, but for the war, would have been engaged in directing its commerce and manufactures … and in filling important position in every sphere of civil life'. You might think the author had a very high opinion of the type of men who became officers in the war, but the fact remains that – almost automatically – these men and those with university degrees, the 'right' background or public school educations would have, but for the war, become managers, civil servants, foreign service administrators, merchants, bankers, diplomats – in short, the men who would have the run the Empire. The men of this class suffered, disproportionally, the highest casualties of the war, especially young junior officers, and Britain needed to find ways of using the remainder who survived more efficiently. Interestingly, the book talks of reaching out to convalescencing and wounded officers to encourage them to study in order to make them 'fit' for their future. The text also refers to changing expectations of civilian life which will be very different to war, even implying that the men will have less money than they did as a second lieutenant (quoted at £280 a year), but warns there will be no 'soft jobs' after the war.

In effect, the book pushes training, study and education (especially university education) for the ex-officer as the way forward for Britain, as if many of the men at whom the book is aimed had never had the opportunity before. It even explains what a university is and how to build a career by choosing the right basic degree (it recommends engineering or chemistry in particular); students of today take note. 'At the outset, realise what a University is … if you have brains enough, you can obtain at a university the right to put certain letters after your name … And such letters undoubtedly have, in some circumstances, a certain commercial value'. Hopefully this is still true. It does warn, however, that a 'BA [is] sometimes overrated in the teaching profession'!

The rest of the book details various courses and degrees around the country at various universities (Derby is not among them as it did not have a university then), and provides details of professions that required degrees and what skills were needed. Although Derby did not have a university and Nottingham was only a 'University College', the book provides valuable insight into the East Midlands and how the authorities perceived its value as a region at the time. Nottingham was considered to be a good place to study engineering, geography and mine surveying and mining for example, as well as being good for dental surgery, chemistry and law (with degrees being issued via examination by the University of London). Derby and Derbyshire is discussed as having coalfields of 'exceptional purity' known to be one 'of the most highly-prized seams in the world'. Derby itself is regarded as a 'great railway centre'.

The book also deals with home study and correspondence courses and discusses well-known institutions such as the Worker's Educational Association (WEA), still going strong today. Although the Open University did not exist in 1918, its future need can be seen in this book.

Finally it discusses some institutions as possible career opportunities, such as the Church of England (as priests), the post-war conditions of the armed forces and the 'mercantile marine' (or what we call the Merchant Navy), the civil service, educational professions, medicine, insurance and law. Most interesting is the short section on the armed forces that was clearly written before the war was over: 'the whole question of entry into the Navy, the Army and the Royal Air Force, must obviously be reconsidered and depend upon the state of the world when peace is finally concluded, and upon conditions which are even now changing.' The book is clearly intended for officers leaving, not young men joining the army for the first time. It suggests there used to be opportunities for ex-officers on the strength of that virtue alone (prison governors, country constables etc.), but not anymore (presumably due to the large numbers suddenly in this position), and not without training or qualifications.

For the ordinary soldier, things were a lot different. It was not until 1919 that soldiers began to be demobilised and dismissed from service (or 'demobbed' as it was and still is commonly called). Men with important industrial skills (miners, for example) were released early and those who had volunteered early in the war were given priority treatment, leaving the conscripts until last. Despite this, most servicemen were back in civilian life by the end of 1919. At first, some soldiers were used in Austria and Germany as occupation forces, similar to that after the end of the Second World War, but not for as long a period. Some men also chose to stay in the Regular Army after the war. From our point of view that might seem strange; how anyone, after years of horror (as we have been taught) could and should want to stay and carry on, is alien to us. The reasons for men of all social backgrounds to join the army were as varied then as they are today, but the army of 1919 was highly trained and experienced, paid well and offered 'career' opportunities and stability in trades that perhaps were not available in civilian life. There is also the possibility that some during the war enjoyed the order and direct purpose that military life offered, as indeed it offers similar satisfaction to those who pursue a career in the armed forces today.

Every soldier was medically examined and given Army Form Z22, which allowed him to make a claim for any form of disability arising from his military service, before he left his regiment or unit. He was also given an Army Form Z44 (Plain Clothes Form) and a Certificate of Employment, showing what he had done in the army, Army Form Z18. A Dispersal Certificate recorded personal and military information. There were rules about bringing money back into the country from France or Italy and they were expected to change the money at a post office. The soldier would spend some time in a transit camp near the coast before being sent home.

On arrival in England, the soldier would move to a Dispersal Centre, which was often nothing more than a hutted or tented camp. Here he received further certificates (Army Form Z11) and a railway warrant or ticket to his home station. He also obtained an 'Out-of-work Donation Policy', which insured him against unavoidable unemployment of up to twenty-six weeks in the twelve months following 'demob'. In addition, he received an

The discharge certificate for John Wesley Outram MM, showing regiment (Derbyshire Yeomanry), medal entitlement, job and various dates. (© 2013 Derby Museum Collection, 2004-986/7)

advance of pay, a fortnight's ration book and also a voucher – Army Form Z50 – for the return of his greatcoat to a railway station during his leave. He could choose to have either a clothing allowance of 52s and 6d or be provided with a suit of plain clothes. His final leave began the day after he was dispersed. He left to go home, still in uniform and with his steel helmet and greatcoat.

The certificate of employment for J.W. Outram MM listing ranks, jobs and specialist training he received. (© 2013 Derby Museum Collection, 2004-986/11)

(8 17 5) W6938—GD1389 5,000,000 10/18 HWV(P598)   Army Form Z. 18.

CERTIFICATE OF EMPLOYMENT DURING THE WAR.
(To be completed for, and handed to, each soldier).

A soldier is advised to send a copy rather than the original when corresponding with a prospective employer.

It is particularly important that an apprentice whose apprenticeship has been interrupted by Military Service should have recorded on this form any employment in a trade similar to his own on which he has been engaged during such Military Service.

Regtl. No. *75124*   Rank *Sgt*

Surname (block letters) *OUTRAM*

Christian Names in full *JOHN WESLEY*

Regt. *Corps of Dragoons*   Unit *1/1 Derbyshire Yeomanry*

1. **Regimental Employment.**

	Nature of.	Period.
(a)	*Lance Corpl*	From *July 1913* To *Aug 1914*
(b)	*Corporal*	" *Aug 1914* " *Feb 1915*
(c)	*Lance Sergeant*	" *Feb 1915* " *Apl 1916*
(d)	*Sergeant*	" *Apl 1916* " *26/2/19*

*2. **Trade or calling before Enlistment** (as shown in A. B. 64).

Postman   GROUP 55   CODE 441

3. **Courses of Instruction and Courses in Active Service Army Schools, and certificates, if any.**

(a) *H.M. Gun   Army Machine Gun*

(b) *School   B S F*

(c) _____

(d) _____

* The trade or calling must be filled in by the O.C. Unit from the Appendix to Special Army Order No. 6, of 21st October, 1918 (329 of November, 1918).

[P.T.O.

Returning soldiers received little practical help after this and they were expected to put themselves back in civilian life and find new jobs, perhaps in their old firms that had moved on technologically, or now employed women instead. With the recession of the 1920s and depression of the 1930s looming, it was no wonder a lot of men found these prospects daunting.

Army Form
Z11; the Army
Protection Certificate.
(© 2013 Derby
Museum Collection,
2004-986/5)

PROTECTION CERTIFICATE AND CERTIFICATE OF IDENTITY
(SOLDIER NOT REMAINING WITH THE COLOURS)

Photograph of
J.W. Outram MM
of the Derbyshire
Yeomanry.
(© 2013 Derby
Museum Collection,
2003-188/61)

Military life was not completely over either, and demobbed men found themselves as 'Class Z Reservists', which was created by an army order of 3 December 1918. There were fears that Germany would not accept the terms of any peace treaty, and therefore the British Government decided it would be wise to be able to quickly recall trained men in the eventuality of the reopening of hostilities. Soldiers who were being demobilised, particularly those who had agreed to serve 'for the duration', were at first posted to Class Z. They returned to civilian life but with an obligation to return if called upon. The Z Reserve was finally abolished on 31 March 1920.

Shell Shock

No other war or conflict in the twentieth century has been associated more with what was called 'shell shock', or what would now be known as 'combat stress' or 'post-traumatic stress disorder', than the First World War. Previous wars were horrific, with massive civilian casualties (the seventeenth-century English Civil War for example), atrocities, disease and death (the nineteenth-century Crimean War had higher casualty rates than the First World War). However, the experiences of the volunteer or conscripted First World War soldier are widely considered more traumatic and horrific than any other war either before or since (notwithstanding the horrors of the Holocaust in the Second World War). This is largely due to the scale of mechanised death, while still (at first) using the tactics of the previous century, such as cavalry or walking in lines. Chemical warfare, a horror born in the First World War that is still regarded with fear today, was an ever-present threat, as was the possibility of complete destruction and vaporisation by explosive ordnance, and the 'wiping out' of entire companies in one day. Perhaps it was the lack of achievement and the perceived pointlessness of the whole thing that led to a creeping anguish and trauma on the psyche

It is believed that by the end of the war over 80,000 cases of shell shock had passed through British Army medical facilities. By 1939, some 120,000 British ex-servicemen had received final awards for primary psychiatric disability – about 15 per cent of all pensioned disabilities.

of the ordinary soldier. It is no exaggeration that much of what soldiers saw was 'hell on earth', and no wonder – especially when you throw in 'survivors' guilt' – the soldiers who did survive experienced psychological problems and mental health concerns well into the 1920s and 1930s.

Symptoms of shell shock included a sense of helplessness and panic, the inability to sleep, walk or talk and the slowing of reactions. Other signs included dizziness, tinnitus and amnesia. There were other symptoms as well; not everyone was the same and many of these we might recognise as 'stress' symptoms today, such as insomnia, anxiety, loss of appetite and the inability to relax. The immediate effect of any or all of these on the soldier in the front lines (and therefore fighting effectiveness) is easy to see, but the longer term effects on society as a whole over a decade or two is harder to judge.

At the beginning of the war, shell shock was poorly understood and was often seen as lack of moral fibre or as cowardice. Early in the war, the BEF reported 'nervous and mental shock' symptoms similar to that experienced after head wounds, but where none were present. The term itself comes from a 1915 *The Lancet* article linking the noise, concussion force and fumes of artillery shells with cases of mental fatigue, and saw the condition as a physical disorder rather than a psychological one.

As the war progressed, the medical profession realised some of the symptoms had nothing to do with artillery, but still differentiated between those who had a 'physical' reason for their behaviour and those who did not. By 1917, a greater understanding developed, largely due to the scale of the problem: it is estimated that about 40 per cent of soldiers at the Battle of the Somme in 1916 displayed some symptoms. Efforts at treatment included 'a few days' rest' prescribed by the local medical officer, talking to the soldier (akin to what we might call counselling today) and close monitoring. It was increasingly seen to be better to see the men as having psychological problems rather than physiological, as it was perceived that the psychologically sick were technically 'uninjured' and therefore easier to return to the front to continue fighting.

Severe cases were treated at local casualty clearing stations and, if symptoms persisted, a casualty might be evacuated to one of four dedicated psychiatric centres which had been set up behind the lines, and were labelled as 'Not Yet Diagnosed Nervous' (NYDN) pending further investigation by medical specialists.

As the war continued and then ended, the British Army and the government considered how to implement changes to treatment, which in turn affected the development of psychiatry in the UK. In 1922, the British Government produced a report of the War Office Committee of Enquiry into shell shock which had a number of recommendations for the future, including what to do in 'forward areas' and behind the lines, such as setting up neurological centres and treatment protocols in base hospitals:

A postcard of nurses and wounded serviceman (cats were used for company and therapy), addressed to Mr J. Richardson of 5 Livingstone Road, Derby; dated 30 January 1917. (© 2013 Derby Museums collection 1985-286/181)

No soldier should be allowed to think that loss of nervous or mental control provides an honourable avenue of escape from the battlefield, and every endeavour should be made to prevent slight cases leaving the battalion or divisional area, where treatment should be confined to provision of rest and comfort for those who need it and to heartening them for return to the front line.

New treatments were considered, including what we would call psychotherapy and physical therapy as well as hypnotic sleep – even baths. A new air of care prevailed, as is evident in the Report of the War Office Comittee of Enquiry into 'Shell-Shock' published in 1922: 'If the patient is unfit for further military service, it is considered that every endeavour should be made to obtain for him suitable employment on his return to active life.' Returning to the 'fighting line' was also discouraged under certain conditions.

There were 240,000 British soldiers court martialed and 3,080 death sentences handed down for desertion and cowardice, but in only 346 cases was this carried out. Records show that 266 British soldiers were executed for 'desertion', 18 for 'cowardice' and 14 for other offences like disobeying a command. On 7 November 2006, they were all posthumously pardoned.

Women Return to the Home

By the 1921 census, the employment of women in Derby was back to roughly 30 per cent, almost the same as the pre-war rate, so from that basis alone it appears that no progress had been made on the issue of equality for women in the workplace. There were a number of reasons for this. Despite huge causalities, men did return from the war and were put back into work, often with their old employers. Women who had been employed during the war were often contracted for 'the duration of the war' and therefore immediately displaced. There is evidence that this was done quickly too; in their peace celebrations for 1919, Derby Corporation states that tram services would be suspended to allow 'discharged and demobilised men' who made up over half their workforce to take part, indicating that returning men rapidly displaced women employees (*Derby Daily Telegraph*, 16 July 1919).

Women workers were often less 'unionised' before the war, working part-time or in smaller firms without unions. The unions themselves were often 'anti-women', in the sense that many did not allow female membership (although the number of female members of unions increased hugely during the war, it was not equal to the number of women who entered work). All this added up to little protection for employment rights or pay. In addition, certain social and practical benefits (such as being encouraged to work 'for the war effort' or day nurseries for working mothers) ended. In addition, the men themselves complained that women were taking their jobs and, to make matters even more difficult, some women campaigned against married women working. Isobel M. Pazzey of Woolwich wrote to the *Daily Herald* in October 1919: 'No decent man would allow his wife to work, and no decent woman would do it if she knew the harm she was doing to the widows and single girls who are looking for work.' It took some decades and another war for these attitudes to fall away.

The war created a number of legacies for working women. Firstly, the types of occupation and employment available did increase due to war, especially in the numbers of women who went into nursing. Secondly, the war seemed to hasten the fall in the demand for domestic service. Before the war, domestic service and domestic labour in hotels presented a high percentage (about 13 per cent nationally) of the total number of employed women. Due to simple changing attitudes and technological introductions of new machines and devices (what used to be referred to as 'domestic appliances' but what we might call 'white goods' today), designed to reduce the need for domestic labour or at least make it quicker, meant that middle-class demand for servants was falling. Many who were domestic servants before the war moved into 'new' professions such as bus and tram drivers during the war, and therefore were not available or did not want to make themselves available for domestic labour afterwards. Secondly, the rapidly growing civil service needed people to fill clerical posts – such as secretarial roles – due to advances in technology, and women were considered the best choice. Younger women in particular benefitted from these opportunities, as they now had increased freedom, as well as greater earning potential.

The one great legacy of the war era for women has long been cited as the right to vote as a 'reward' for war work. However, this is not as clear-cut as it seems. This was granted for women for the first time in 1918 for those who were over 30 and who held property, which is a rather narrow qualification by our standards and one at odds with who actually did the majority of that 'war work', the young single women, in the first place. The war was not the only reason for women to receive the vote; in fact, it was just one of a number of factors which led to change. Lobbying by the feminist movement had been going on for decades, and adding this to the Labour Party's desire to widen the franchise meant that their wish was granted. Even the Suffragette movement's decision at the outbreak of war to cease their more aggressive and radical militant tactics in favour of patriotism helped. Finally, it was necessary in 1917 to hold an election, and this caused the government to rethink the situation. With so many men away and no longer legally able to vote as they had not been a resident in the UK for twelve months (fighting in France did not count), there was a need to change the rules. Seeing their chance, Millicent Fawcett and the National Union of Women's Suffrage Societies persuaded the Liberal leader, H.H. Asquith, to grant a minority of women the vote by drawing attention to the work of women during the war. But it was not until 1928 that women over the age of 21 were finally allowed to vote. In effect, granting women over 30 the vote meant that in 1918, 8.5 million women were enfranchised, or 40 per cent of the female population. In 1928, this was boosted to 15 million, or 53 per cent of total number of women.

Postscript

Legacy

Remembrance

With the war over, the business of remembrance began and up and down the country people decided how best to do this. Many companies (such as the Post Office or banks and insurance companies) decided to erect memorials or have brass or bronze plaques made to those men from their firms who had fallen, and nearly all villages and towns raised an 'official' memorial to the dead, often in some central spot. There were also many smaller and more personal memorials, plaques and crosses in local parish churches, village halls and meeting places, paid for by individuals, societies and clubs. Most use similar phrases and words: 'To the brave men of _____ who gave their lives in the Great War' or 'Lest We Forget', and unlike the habit of referring to the conflict today, the war is recorded as being 1914 to 1919, not 1918. Nearly all list the names of those who died, who 'made the supreme sacrifice, and those of us who are living under the freedom purchased at the cost

Drawing of the Midland Railway company memorial designed by Sir Edwin L. Lutyens, RA. (Derby Museums collection 1978-90 © 2013)

of these lives cannot allow the memory of their devotion to die'. It sometimes took many years for a local committee to decide on the scope of a memorial and raise funds for it. It was often well into the 1920s before many of these appeared, and some were not erected until the 1930s. Many of the First World War memorials were eventually co-opted into being Second World War memorials, by adding new elements, plaques or additional carvings.

Most of the larger memorials had lists of names, mostly alphabetical, and often indicating regiment or service branches. Occasionally, you can see additional names squeezed in at the bottom out of alphabetical order. These are usually men who died of their wounds shortly after the list was approved, or died much later, but who had relatives who canvassed the erecting committees to add their name.

One such large memorial in Derby is the Cenotaph, erected by the Midland Railway near the train station in honour of the 2,833 men who died. This was paid for by the company and designed by Sir Edwin L. Lutyens, RA, who also designed the National Memorial erected at Westminister. A book was also published, entitled *In Remembrance of the Brave Men of the Midland Railway who Gave their Lives in the Great War 1914–1919* (Derby Museum Reference, 1978–90). This book lists every man, their role within the company, the station at which they were based and which department they worked in, as well as their military rank and regiment in the war. The book sets out the rationale for the memorial:

> [Lutyens] design expresses the triumphant end of the war, as well as the sadness and sorrow it entailed, and is intended to embody the whole meaning of those troubled years which have bequeathed to us the memory of so many good lives lost and stout hearts which no longer beat. It marks the victory which crowned their whole efforts, and the pride with which the Midland Company can truly affirm- 'our men did not a little to that end'.

Note the imperialistic and patriotic language here: loss, yes, but the emphasis is clearly on 'victory' and 'triumph' rather than the tragic waste of lives that is nowadays associated with the First World War.

It is interesting to note that a copy of the book was sent to the families and relatives of the fallen and that the company was willing to provide free travel to those who wished to visit the memorial (widows, parents and children), as long as they applied to the general manager. In the foreword, much is made of those who did not fight but served in other ways (as drivers in Britain, for example), nevertheless displaying 'the same spirit of patriotic devotion, offered their utmost to the nation in the hour of her deep need' and, in particular, those women who served on the platforms, sheds, offices and workshops and also 'played their part in the successful working of the Midland Railway,

22,941 employees of the Midland Railway served in the war (30.9 per cent of the workforce), of which 2,833 were killed (12 per cent). The total number of officers and men wounded or invalided was 7,068, while 738 officers and men were taken prisoner. 32 Military Crosses were awarded, along with 1 bar; 341 Military Medals were awarded as well as 17 bars.

and, in so doing, made their contribution to the final success which crowned the united efforts of the Allied Forces'.

Also recognised were the 'unmistakable signs' of mental and physical trauma with which the survivors would have to live, and the general manager extends a particular 'tribute to their courage and fortitude, and extend to them the assurance of our sympathy'.

Another way to honour the war dead was remembrance books; these were hand written in beautiful calligraphy, with the names and dates of the fallen, and they were often produced by the regiments in which the men served. For example, the remembrance book for the Sherwood Foresters can be seen on display at Derby Museum and Art Gallery in their military gallery ('The Soldier's Story') and individual names can be seen on request by appointment. A similar book for the Derbyshire Yeomanry can be seen at Derby Cathedral.

Derby City Council keeps an eye on the various war memorials around the city and it is always best to contact the Environmental Protection Office if you think any memorial is at risk of loss or damage. There is a register based on an extensive survey undertaken in the late 1990s. This survey also contains Second World War memorials.

The survey gives a broad view of the kinds of memorials that were made and by whom. For example, two bronze plaques were placed on the gateposts of Allestree Recreation Ground in 1930 'as a memorial to the men of this village'; they cost £20 (paid by public subscription) and were unveiled by Captain Guy Gisborne. Another small stone plaque was fitted in the exterior wall of the Roebuck Inn on Amy Street with the words: 'In proud and glorious memory of our boys. Their name liveth for evermore. Greater love hath no man than this that a man lay

The remembrance book of the Sherwood Foresters war dead. This can be seen at Derby Museum and Art Gallery in the Soldiers' Story gallery. (© 2013 Mike Galer)

down his life for his friends.' Note the word 'friends' here; not 'King and Country'.

Other small memorials were placed in the Church Army Mission Hall; Bridgegate to Jacob Rivers VC; Hasting Street Schools; Derby Cathedral; Chaddesden Memorial Hall; Broadway Baptist church; Christ church, Normanton Road; Holy Trinity Church, London Road; Derby Locomotive Works and the Wagon and Carriage Works; Derby Royal Infirmary; Derby Station; Osmaston Road/Shaftesbury Street; Osmaston Road, Baptist Church; St Michael's church; St John's church; Bridge Street and many others.

The 1914–18 Roll of Honour in D Coach Finishing Shop at the Midland Railway Carriage and Wagon Works, off Litchurch Lane. (© 2004 Derby Museums collection DMAG001964)

Other memorials were larger, such as the official memorial at the Market Place in Crich. The Market Place memorial is a large stone cross with a bronze figure of a woman and child entitled 'The Great War 1914–1918', with a later Second World War inscription. The memorial was designed by Charles Clayton Thompson and sculpted by Arthur G. Walker. Unveiled on 11 November 1924 by Alderman Ling, Chairman of the War Memorial Committee, it was dedicated by the Bishop of Southwell. During the unveiling ceremony, the mother of Jacob Rivers VC laid a wreath at the foot of the memorial. Prior to

the permanent memorial, there was a temporary wooden cross which was erected on 25 April 1920.

In Commonwealth countries, the memorial day for all wars is 'Remembrance Day' (also known as Poppy Day), held on the 11 November (with a memorial service in most towns and cities on the following Sunday – Remembrance Sunday - usually held near the official war memorials of said town and city) each year to recall the end of hostilities of the First World War and to remember those of the armed forces who have died in the line of duty.

The day was dedicated by King George V on 7 November 1919 as a day of remembrance for members of the armed forces who were killed during the war, and the first official Remembrance Day was held in the grounds of Buckingham Palace on the morning of 11 November 1919. The red poppy has become an enduring emblem of Remembrance Day, due to the poem 'In Flanders Fields' by John Alexander McCrae, in reference to the brilliant blood-red poppies that bloomed across some of the worst battlefields of Flanders.

CASUALTY RATES

Official figures for casualties for the First World War vary and have changed over time. The first official 'final and corrected' casualty figures for the British Army, including the Territorial Force (not including allied British Empire forces), were issued on 10 March 1921 and covered the period from 4 August 1914 to 30 September 1919. This stated that 573,507 were 'killed in action, died from wounds and died of other causes' and 254,176 were missing, less 154,308 released prisoners – a total of 673,375 dead and missing. There were a further 1,643,469 wounded also listed in the report. *The Statistics of the Military Effort of the British Empire During the Great War 1914–1920*, published by the War Office March in 1922, lists 908,371 soldiers that were killed in action, died of wounds, died as prisoners of war and were missing in action from 4 August 1914 to 31 December 1920, plus a further 14,661 for the Merchant Navy.

The current view by the Commonwealth War Graves Commission is that, between 4 August 1914 and 31 August 1921, the total dead numbered 1,115,597 (UK and former colonies, 886,939; Undivided India, 74,187; Canada, 64,976; Australia, 61,966; New Zealand, 18,052; South Africa, 9,477).

For the British Empire in total, with around 8.6 million men mobilised, this equates to a death rate of approximately 12 per cent overall (17 per cent for its officers and – it is believed – 20 per cent of those who served for former pupils of Eton school).

At a local level, 22,941 employees of Midland Railway fought in the war in various regiments, with 2,833 killed (12.35 per cent). For the Sherwood Foresters (Notts. & Derby) Regiment, 11,409 soldiers lost their lives in the First World War, out of over 140,000 who served in total (around 8 per cent). Conversely, the Derbyshire Yeomanry (who were not deployed for combat until 1915) lost 79 men out of a total regiment (including home service battalions) of over 1700 (4.6 per cent death casualty rate).

German stretcher bearers, likely prisoners of war, under supervision by Allied troops, somewhere in France 1915–18. (© 2008 Derby Museums)

The Lost Generation

The term the 'Lost Generation' is generally credited to Ernest Hemingway, who in turn credited someone else, but he certainly popularised it through his 1926 novel *The Sun Also Rises*. It refers to the young who came of age (achieved adulthood) during the war and shortly after. In Britain, the term was originally used for those who died in the war, and often implicitly referred to upper-class casualties who were perceived to have died disproportionately (17 per cent as opposed to 12 per cent for ordinary ranks), implying that the country had been robbed of a future elite. Many felt the youth and the future of the nation had been lost or damaged, including many notable casualties that may have gone on to greater things, for example the poets Isaac Rosenberg, Rupert Brooke and Wilfred Owen, composer George Butterworth and physicist Henry Moseley.

In a narrow sense it refers to an artistic and literary movement in Europe, made up of artists, thinkers and writers, many of whom had served in combat during the war or were involved in protests for and against it, such as Gertrude Stein, Ernest Hemingway, Ezra Pound and F. Scott Fitzgerald. As a result, they had a deep sense of disillusionment and mistrust created by the violence of the war, seeing it as senseless brutality that destroyed the innocence that dominated society at the turn of the twentieth century.

Unlike most 'ordinary' soldiers coming back from the war, these writers and thinkers were often middle-class in origin – or at least moderately wealthy in the case of the Americans – and lived what might be called bohemian lifestyles. They challenged conventional attitudes about appropriate behaviour, especially for women, and challenged acceptable expressions of morality, especially around sexuality. Their work often questioned society as a whole.

However, in a wider sense, the phrase is often used when discussing the high level of youth unemployment and disillusionment that many young people experienced in the post-war years. Lingering effects of wounds, shell shock, other psychological problems (including 'survivor's guilt') and the need to rationalise the war into something more than just a pointless conflict all took their toll. Despite perhaps the reality that the war did not change a lot geographically or even politically, many young men who had lost friends and relatives tried to give meaning to their deaths by romanticising their sacrifice into something more. The survivor had to believe that their dead comrade died heroically and justly in order to function. This gave rise to a myth that the lost generation that perished was somehow 'better' than those who survived, who felt less heroic and less noble than their dead friends. This feeling was not helped by the constant rhetoric that 'the nation's best had been lost', hardly helpful to those still alive who felt that society viewed them as less than the best. It is no wonder then that a lot of young men struggled in social situations, found it difficult to adjust to new working practices and wrestled with family life (domestic abuse and violence rose in the 1920s and '30s, as did alcohol abuse). However, many did thrive – acquired new jobs, started businesses, married, had children – and were more than ready in many cases to serve again in the Second World War as air raid wardens or in the Home Guard and, in some cases, in combat. Perhaps it would take a new war to erase the scars of the old.

Final Thoughts

Derby no doubt benefited industrially and economically from the businesses that thrived during the war, such as Rolls-Royce and British Celanese, but this is a poor substitute for the many lives lost and many more who were changed forever. Many of these businesses provided work for thousands of people for the next 100 years and, in the case of Rolls-Royce, are still going strong well into the twenty-first century. Women benefited too from the war, with social empowerment and new work opportunities. Despite this, and rightly so, the First World War will always be remembered as a 'pointless' war with needless slaughter and destruction, with no clear outcome.

It is difficult to do full justice to the tens of thousands of Derby and Derbyshire men and women who served and sacrificed so much in the First World War; each with their own individual stories and concerns. It is impossible to mention them all. This book is dedicated to their memory.

A photograph of an unknown young soldier of the Derbyshire Yeomanry. We will never know if this man survived the war. (© 2013 Derby Museums collection 1992/170)

SOURCES

All photographs are from the collections of Derby Museums, except where indicated. Newspaper headline scans and pictures are courtesy of Derby Local Studies Library and used with permission of the *Derby Daily Telegraph*. All scanning, digital editing and other preparations of original photographic prints, postcards, letters, books, articles, objects and artefacts was undertaken by the author Mike Galer and the above resources remain copyright of Derby Museum Trust. All colour outside photographs of places, memorials and similar are copyright of Mike Galer.

Newspapers and archives: the *Derby Daily Telegraph*, *Derby Mercury* and other newspapers can be found at Derby Local Studies Library as can cuttings, articles, journals and official reports such as the 1911 and 1921 census returns and summaries. Other material such as letters, postcards and diaries are part of Derby Museums collections and examined there.

The 'Derbyshire Red Book Almanack & Annual Register', printed by Bemrose of Derby of 1914, 1915 and 1916 (Derby local studies reference number A305) is a good source of local information and facts, as are the *Kelly's Directories*.

For the Zeppelin raid, the best source is *Airs from Heaven* by John Hook, 1994. A copy can be found at Derby Local Studies Library.

Chapter 6: *In Remembrance of the Brave Men of the Midland Railway who Gave their Lives in the Great War 1914–1919* was printed by Bemrose & Sons Ltd, Derby, in 1921 – the copy used was part of the Derby Museum collection.

A Record of Opportunity as to Careers and Training was published November 1918 by the Appointments Department of the Ministry of Labour, Victoria Street, London, and was printed by Alabaster, Passmore and Sons, Ltd, London – the copy used was part of the Derby Museum collection.

Trooper Cooling's diary is an artefact accessioned by Derby Museums and transcriptions are used by permission of the transcriber, Martin Gillott who retains copyright.

The 'Dyke' postcards are a set of sixty-six postcards sent by Private A.H. Dyke, 1914–16, to his wife and children and represents a remarkable insight, though one-sided, of the war. Albert was killed on 6 June 1916, while serving with the Sherwood Foresters on the Somme.

Where possible, accession numbers of physical objects have been provided within the picture caption. Please contact Derby Museums if you want to see any of these or have further questions.

About the Author

Dr Mike Galer was Senior Collection Officer and Curator of the 9th/12th Lancers Museum at Derby Museums for seven years. He is currently the General Manager of Crich Tramway Village and National Tramway Museum.

Great War Britain:
The First World War at Home

Luci Gosling

After the declaration of war in 1914, the conflict dominated civilian life for the next four years. Magazines quickly adapted without losing their gossipy essence: fashion jostled for position with items on patriotic fundraising, and court presentations were replaced by notes on nursing. The result is a fascinating, amusing and uniquely feminine perspective of life on the home front.

978 0 7524 9188 2

The Workers' War:
British Industry and the First World War

Anthony Burton

The First World War didn't just rock the nation in terms of bloodshed: it was a war of technological and industrial advances. Working Britain experienced change as well: with the men at war, it fell to the women of the country to keep the factories going. Anthony Burton explores that change.

978 0 7524 9886 7

Visit our website and discover many other First World War books.

www.thehistorypress.co.uk/first-world-war